ALGEBRA

BY
DON BLATTNER AND MYRL SHIREMAN

ISBN 10-digit: 1-58037-057-8
13-digit: 978-1-58037-057-8

Printing No. CD-1874

Mark Twain Media, Inc., Publishers
Distributed by Carson-Dellosa Publishing Company, Inc.

Table of Contents

Introduction

Algebra is increasingly becoming a required course in the curriculum of many schools. Algebra is also the keystone course students need as they begin developing the mathematics skills needed in today's world. However, many students enrolled in today's algebra classes will not succeed without many opportunities to practice the skills required for success in algebra. The skills emphasized in this book are those that are basic to understanding the major concepts taught in Algebra I.

Each skill introduced is followed by examples, the opportunity to practice the skill, and a short quiz over the concept. The emphasis of the material in each lesson is on understanding and using the basic concept in the lesson rather than giving broad coverage. This format is followed because the success of many students depends on ample explanation followed by practice lessons that allow the student to gain confidence in using the skills.

This book may be used by parents or teachers as a primer prior to introducing the basic concepts that will be needed in algebra. It is also designed as a supplement to be used by classroom teachers to provide extra practice on some of the key skills taught in Algebra I.

Name ______________________________ Date ______________________________

Understanding Number Systems

In order to study algebra, one must understand the number system. Read the definition for each of the types of numbers and complete the exercise below each definition. Fill in the blanks with the numbers that should follow for the given definition. Remember each of the sets of numbers is infinite.

Counting numbers: Sometimes called natural numbers, they are 1, 2, 3, 4, 5, 6…

1) 1, 2, 3, 4,___ ,___ ,___ ,___ ,___ ,___ ,___ ,___ ,___ ,___ …

2) ___,___,___, 54, 55, 56, 57,___,___,___,___,___,___…

3) 1234,_____ ,_____ ,_____ ,_____ , 1239,_____ ,_____ …

Whole numbers: The whole numbers are 0, 1, 2, 3, 4, 5, 6…

4) 0, 1, 2, 3, 4, 5, 6,___ ,___ ,___ ,___ ,___ ,___ ,___ ,___ ,___ ,___ ,___ ,___ …

5) ___ ,___ ,___ ,___ ,___ ,___ , 30, 31,___ ,___ ,___ , 35,___…

6) 223, 224,___ ,___ ,___ ,___ ,___ ,___ ,___ …

Integer numbers: Integers are whole numbers together with their negatives

…-6, -5, -4, -3, -2, -1, 0, 1, 2, 3, 4, 5, 6…

7) …___,___ ,___ ,___ ,___ ,___ ,___ ,___ , -4, -3, -2, -1, 0, 1, 2, 3, 4,___ ,___ ,___ ,___ ,

___ ,___ ,___ ,___ ,___ ,___ ,___ ,___ …

8) …- 10,009,_____ ,_____ ,_____ ,_____ ,_____ ,_____ ,_____ ,_____ , - 10,000…

In each of the above examples, three dots (…) were used at the beginning or at the end of the set of numbers. These three dots are called **ellipsis points** and in mathematics they are the symbol for the term **infinite**. Infinite means without end. When used in conjunction with a number or a set of numbers, the ellipsis points indicate that the numbers could go on forever. For example, 6… means that the numbers are infinite. There is no end to the numbers that could follow the numeral six. If you started counting you could not count all of the numbers that would follow.

None of the above number systems include fractions. When you are solving problems and you are limited to **counting numbers**, **whole numbers,** or **integers,** there are no fractions.

Name ________________________ Date ________________________

Real Numbers

A common term used in mathematics is **real number system.** The real number system was developed by mathematicians to include fractions. Here is a quick review of fractions. **Fractions** have a numerator and a denominator. The **numerator** is the number above the line, and the **denominator** is the number below the line.

The numerator may be any integer. The denominator may be any integer except zero (0). In the fraction $\frac{3}{4}$, the three (3) is the numerator, and the four (4) is the denominator. The 3 and 4 are both integers, and the denominator is not zero.

When any number is divided by zero there is no possible answer. For that reason the definition of a fraction states that the denominator of a fraction cannot be zero.

Example:

$\frac{3}{0}$ is not a fraction because the denominator is zero.

Attempt to solve the problems below. Divide to the fourth decimal place.

1) $\frac{3}{0} = 3 \div 0 =$ __________ 2) $\frac{5}{0} = 5 \div 0 =$ __________ 3) $\frac{0}{2} = 0 \div 2 =$ __________

Look at the following numbers. Circle the ones that are fractions.

4) $\frac{5}{6}$ 5) $\frac{6}{7}$ 6) $\frac{3}{4}$ 7) $\frac{2}{0}$ 8) $\frac{5}{0}$ 9) $\frac{1}{9}$ 10) $\frac{6}{50}$

***Real numbers* are sometimes rational numbers, and sometimes they are irrational numbers.**

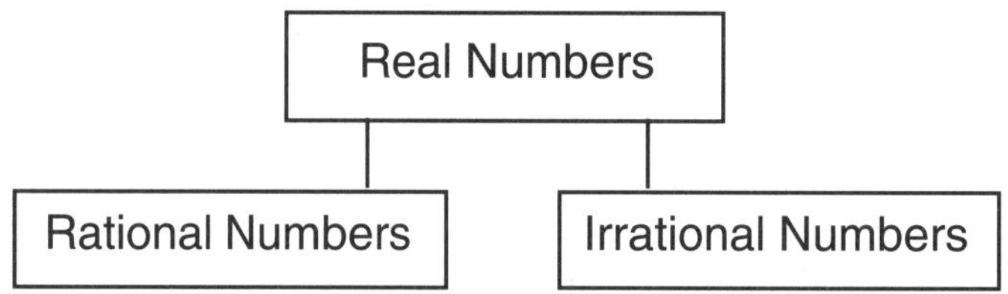

***Rational numbers* are numbers that can be written as the quotient of fractions.**

Examples:

a) $\frac{3}{4} = 3 \div 4 =$ answer: 0.75

b) $\frac{2}{3} = 2 \div 3 =$ answer: 0.66666666…

Notice the above fractions are quite different. In the first example, the quotient of 0.75 is said to be a **non-repeating** decimal, which means that it cannot be divided any further. In the second example, the answer is a **repeating** decimal. In other words, no matter how long you divided, you would continue to get 0.666… . The ellipsis points (…) indicate that further division would produce the number 6 infinitely. However, both of these fractions are examples of rational numbers since the answers can be written as the quotient of a fraction.

Name ______________________________ Date ____________________________

Quotient Questions

Complete the following. Express each answer as the quotient of the fraction. In the space provided, show all work for finding the answers to Questions 1, 2, and 3. Then use a calculator to find the solutions that are repeating decimals, and write their answers carried to eight places.

1) $\frac{3}{5} = 3 \div 5 =$

2) $\frac{7}{8} = 7 \div 8 =$

3) $\frac{8}{9} = 8 \div 9 =$

You may use your calculator for answering the following.

4) $\frac{1}{6}$ = __÷__ = ________ 5) $\frac{4}{5}$ = __÷__ = ________ 6) $\frac{7}{12}$ = ____________
7) $\frac{3}{7}$ = ____________ 8) $\frac{9}{16}$ = ____________ 9) $\frac{1}{32}$ = ____________
10) $\frac{9}{11}$ = ____________ 11) $\frac{13}{15}$ = ____________ 12) $\frac{5}{1}$ = ____________
13) $\frac{7}{1}$ = ____________ 14) $\frac{56}{1}$ = ____________ 15) $\frac{9}{1}$ = ____________
16) $\frac{88}{1}$ = ____________

17) List the above fractions that are non-repeating or terminating decimals.

a)___ b)___ c)___ d)___ e)___ f)___ g)___ h)___

18) List the above fractions that are repeating decimals.

a)___ b)___ c)___ d)___ e)___

19) Each of the above fractions is a rational number because all of the fractions can be written as a quotient that is either a __________ or a __________ decimal.

20) Any integer can be written as a rational number by writing the integer as the numerator of a fraction and writing the __________ as 1.

Name ______________________________ Date ___________________________

RATIONAL NUMBERS

Rational numbers include ... -6, -5, -4, -3, -2, -1, 0, 1, 2, 3, 4, 5, 6... . Rational numbers also include fractions with a numerator of any integer and a denominator of any integer except zero. Any integer may be written as a fraction with a denominator of one. $\frac{3}{1} = 3$ $\frac{7}{1} = 7$ $\frac{78}{1} = 78$

Each rational number can be located at a precise point on a number line. A number line is divided so that any rational number can be located as a specific point from zero. Any integer can be located on the number line since all integers may be written as a fraction with a denominator of one ($-\frac{5}{1}$, $\frac{5}{1}$, etc).

Example:

$\frac{1}{2}$ is located on the number line by a point exactly half way between 0 and 1.
$-\frac{1}{2}$ is located on the number line by a point exactly half way between 0 and -1.

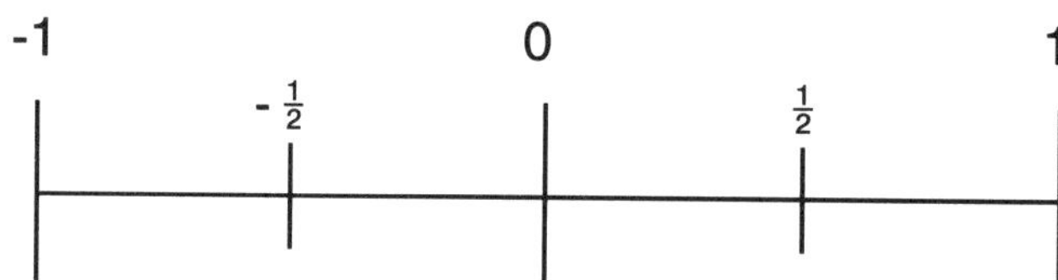

For each of the following rational numbers (fractions), there is a perpendicular line that locates the point on the number line below. Write in the following rational numbers on the correct blanks below the number line.

1) $+\frac{3}{4}$ 2) $+\frac{1}{8}$ 3) $-\frac{3}{4}$ 4) $-\frac{1}{8}$ 5) $+1\frac{1}{2}$ 6) $+1\frac{3}{8}$
7) $-1\frac{1}{2}$ 8) $-1\frac{3}{8}$ 9) $+1\frac{3}{4}$ 10) $-1\frac{3}{4}$ 11) $+\frac{2}{1}$ 12) $+\frac{1}{1}$
13) $-\frac{2}{1}$ 14) $-\frac{1}{1}$

-2 -1 0 +1 +2

Name ______________________________ Date ____________________________

Irrational Numbers

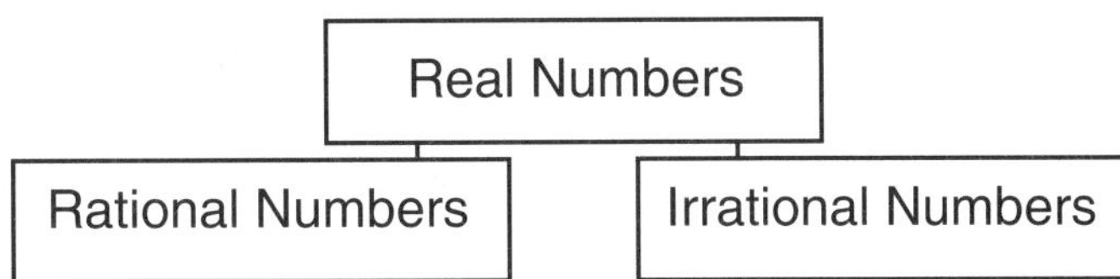

Another kind of real number is called an irrational number.

***Irrational numbers* are infinite, nonrepeating, nonterminating decimals and cannot be located on the number line.** Another way of saying this is that **an irrational number is any real number than cannot be expressed as an integer or a ratio between two integers.**

Example:

Most people have seen the symbol for pi (π). **Pi** is the ratio of the circumference of a circle to its diameter. The decimal for π is 3.14159265... . Note that the ellipsis points indicate that the number is infinite, which means that the numbers in the decimal would go on forever. Also they are non-repeating. In other words, the same numbers are not repeated in the same order as the decimal is carried out further. Therefore, the decimal for π is an **irrational** number.

Finding the square root of numbers is an excellent way to see the difference between rational and irrational numbers. When finding the square root of an integer, the answer is sometimes another integer, which would make the number a rational number. However, many times the answer is a decimal with an infinite number of non-repeating digits. When this occurs, the number is an irrational number.

Extracting the *square root* of a number means finding the number that if multiplied by itself will give the original number.

The square root operation is indicated by a symbol called the **radical sign** ($\sqrt{\ }$). The number under the radical sign is called the **radicand**. A radical sign with a radicand is a **radical**.

Example:

Find the square root of 4. $\sqrt{4} = 2$

Check: $2 \bullet 2 = 4$. So 2 is the square root of 4

Find the square root of 9. $\sqrt{9} = 3$

Check: $3 \bullet 3 = 9$

So 3 is the square root of 9.

In each of the above examples, the square root of the integer is another integer. Remember, an integer can be expressed as a fraction with a denominator of one. Each of

Name ______________________ Date ______________________

Irrational Numbers (continued)

the answers above can be expressed as fractions: $\frac{2}{1}$ and $\frac{3}{1}$. Both are rational numbers that can be located on the number line a specific distance from zero.

Example:

Find the square root of 5. $\sqrt{5} = 2.236067978\ldots$

Check: $2.236067978 \times 2.236067978 = \sqrt{5}$

Although the answer is the square root of 5, the answer is not another integer that can be expressed as a fraction. The answer is a **non-repeating decimal** that cannot be located on the number line. Therefore the answer is an **irrational number**.

To complete the next exercise you will need a calculator. Use the calculator and find the square root for each of the problems. Write the answer on blank a), and on b) indicate if the answer is a **rational or irrational number**. The first one is completed.

1) $\sqrt{4}$ a) 2 ______ b) rational
2) $\sqrt{9}$ a) ______ b) ______
3) $\sqrt{7}$ a) ______ b) ______
4) $\sqrt{11}$ a) ______ b) ______
5) $\sqrt{12}$ a) ______ b) ______
6) $\sqrt{18}$ a) ______ b) ______
7) $\sqrt{17}$ a) ______ b) ______
8) $\sqrt{144}$ a) ______ b) ______
9) $\sqrt{156}$ a) ______ b) ______
10) $\sqrt{125}$ a) ______ b) ______
11) $\sqrt{36}$ a) ______ b) ______
12) $\sqrt{48}$ a) ______ b) ______
13) $\sqrt{49}$ a) ______ b) ______
14) $\sqrt{26}$ a) ______ b) ______

Complete the following diagram using the following terms: **natural numbers, whole numbers, integers, real numbers, rational numbers,** and **irrational numbers.** Place the terms in order in the rectangles beginning with the most complex in the top rectangle.

Real numbers: The rational and irrational numbers together make up the real number system.

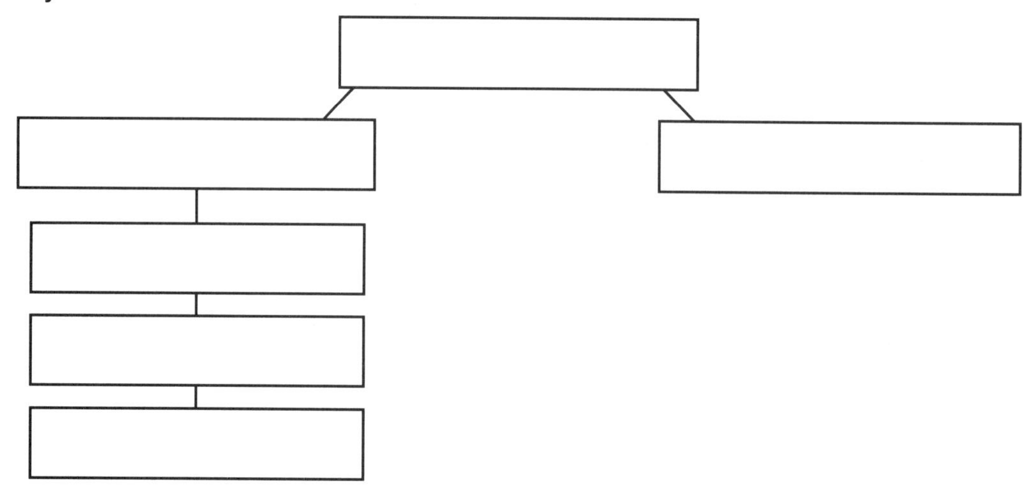

Name ______________________ Date ______________________

Quiz I: Understanding Number Systems

1) The difference between the natural numbers and the whole numbers is the numeral __________.

2) The ____________ numbers include both positive and negative numbers.

3) The ____________ numbers can be written as the quotient of a fraction.

4) The ____________ numbers cannot be written as the quotient of a fraction.

Match the definitions in Column B with the answer in Column A. Write the letter for the correct answer on the blanks in Column A.

Column A	Column B
_____ 5) The numbers ...-2, -1, 0, +1, +2...	A) Whole numbers
_____ 6) The numbers 0, 1, 2, 3, 4, 5...	B) Integer numbers
_____ 7) The numbers 1, 2, 3, 4, 5...	C) Natural numbers
_____ 8) The numbers $\frac{3}{4}$, $\frac{3}{1}$, $\frac{10}{5}$, $\frac{6}{1}$, $\sqrt{9}$...	D) Irrational numbers
_____ 9) The numbers $\sqrt{5}$, $\sqrt{3}$, $\sqrt{8}$, $\frac{5}{7}$...	E) Rational numbers

Identify each of the following as a rational or irrational number. Write rational or irrational in the blank following each number.

10) $\sqrt{4}$ ____________ 11) $\sqrt{7}$ ____________ 12) $\sqrt{25}$ ____________

13) $\frac{2}{3}$ ____________ 14) $\frac{14}{2}$ ____________ 15) $\frac{23}{1}$ ____________

16) 0.800 ____________ 17) 1.414213562... ____________ 18) $\frac{10}{3}$ ____________

Fill in the blanks

19) The quotient of a fraction that is a __________ number always produces a repeating decimal or a non-repeating decimal that is not infinite.

20) An ____________ number cannot be located as a specific point on the number line.

Name ______________________________ Date ______________________________

Adding Positive and Negative Numbers

Understanding how positive and negative numbers are used in addition, subtraction, multiplication, and division is important in the study of algebra. In addition problems, the numbers may all be positive, all negative, or include both positive and negative numbers.

A. To add numbers with like signs, add the numbers and place the sign in front of the sum.

B. To add numbers with unlike signs, subtract the numbers and place the sign of the larger number in front of the sum.

Example:	1) A	2) A	3) B	4) B
	+8	-8	-8	+8
	+ +3	+ -3	+ +3	+ -3
	+11	-11	-5	+5

Refer to A and B above and solve the following problems. Place the letter A or B above each problem to indicate the rule used to solve the problem. The first one is completed.

1) A	2)	3)	4)	5)	6)	7)
+4	-7	-9	+6	+9	-4	+12
+ +2	+ -8	+ +7	+ -4	+ - 5	+ -7	+ +12
+6						

8)	9)	10)	11)	12)	13)
+34	-23	-16	+124	-67	+89
+ - 21	+ -45	+ +18	+ - 23	+ +78	+ +67

14) +9 and -6 = ________ 15) +45 and -67 = ______ 16) +34 and -25 = _______

17) -78 and -65 = ______ 18) +145 and +231 = ____ 19) -14 and +100 = ______

When adding three or more numbers, first add the numbers with like signs and then add the numbers with different signs.

Example: Adding the numbers (-8) + (-7) + (+9)
Add: -8 + -7 = -15 Then add: (-15) + (+9) = -6

Adding the numbers (+12) + (-16) + (-12) + (- 7)
Add: (-16) + (-12) + (-7) = -35 Then add: (-35) + (+12) = -23

Solve the following problems

20)	21)	22)	23)	24)	25)
-3	+8	-23	+34	-78	-6
-9	-18	-18	-89	+12	-23
+5	-24	+9	-78	-45	-7
+ -4	+ +12	+ - 35	+ +4	+ +10	+ -3

Name ______________________________ Date ___________________________

Subtracting Positive and Negative Numbers

Subtraction: In learning about subtracting positive and negative numbers it is important to review the terms **minuend**, **subtrahend,** and **difference**.

Example: Subtract 2 from 8

+8	=	minuend
- +2	=	subtrahend
+6	=	difference

An important rule to remember in subtraction is that the subtrahend and difference when added should equal the minuend. In the example above, 2 + 6 = 8

Subtraction of positive and negative numbers: To subtract using positive and negative numbers you must *change the sign* of the subtrahend and add.

Example: To subtract +8 - +2 change the sign of the subtrahend +8 + -2 and add. +6

Check: Adding the original subtrahend (+2) to the difference (+6) equals +8 (the minuend).

Example: To subtract -8 - +2 change the sign of the subtrahend -8 + -2 and add. -10

Check: Adding the subtrahend (+2) to the difference (-10) equals -8 (the minuend).

Solve the following problems. Change the sign of the subtrahend in "A" and write the new subtrahend in "B". Find the difference and record the difference beneath the line in "B". The first one has been completed.

	A	B
1)	+ 9	+9
	- -5	+ +5
		+14

	A	B
2)	-12	-12
	- +14	+ ___

	A	B
3)	-89	-89
	- ___	+ -18

	A	B
4)	+15	+15
	- -23	+ ___

Check 1) +14 + -5 = +9

Check 2) -____ + ____ = -____

Check 3) -____ + ____ = -____

Check 4) +____ + ____ = +____

5) 8 - (-5) = _____ 6) -23 - (+5) - (+7) = _____ 7) (-16) - (-7) = _____

8) What number must be added to the subtrahend to get the minuend? ____________

Name ______________________________ Date ______________________________

Quiz II: Addition and Subtraction With Positive and Negative Numbers

1) Under column A, write the addition problem (+90) + (-123) in column form in the space below, and solve the problem. Then, under column B, write the terms **addend** and **sum** on the blanks to correctly identify each.

A	B
	____________
___	____________
	____________

Solve the following **addition** problems.

2) +45 + +34	3) -64 + +9	4) +124 + -35	5) +43 + +56	6) -189 + +278	7) +239 + -104	8) -489 + -34

9) Under column A, write the subtraction problem (+ 90) - (- 123) in column form in the space below, and solve the problem. Then, under column B, write the terms **subtrahend**, **difference**, and **minuend** on the blanks to correctly identify each.

A	B
	____________
___	____________
	____________

Solve the following **subtraction** problems.

10) +45 - +34	11) -64 - +9	12) +124 - -35	13) +56 - -43	14) -278 - +189	15) +239 - -104	16) - 489 - -34

Match the term in Column A with the definition in Column B.

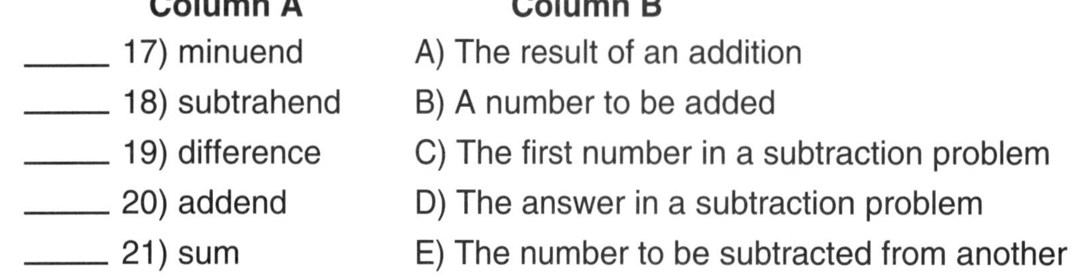

Column A	Column B
_____ 17) minuend	A) The result of an addition
_____ 18) subtrahend	B) A number to be added
_____ 19) difference	C) The first number in a subtraction problem
_____ 20) addend	D) The answer in a subtraction problem
_____ 21) sum	E) The number to be subtracted from another

Name ______________________________ Date ______________________________

Multiplication With Positive and Negative Numbers

When multiplying two numbers with *unlike* signs, multiply as usual and place a *negative* sign in front of the *product*.

Example: (+8) x (-6) = -48 or +8
x -6
-48

When multiplying two numbers with *like* signs, multiply as usual and place a *positive* sign in front of the *product*.

Example: (-8) x (-6) = +48 or -8
x -6
+48

Example: (+8) x (+6) = +48 or +8
x +6
+48

Multiply the following problems. Place the correct sign in front of each product. In the blanks by each problem state the rule used to determine the sign for the product.

1) +8
x +4 ______________________________
____

2) -80
x +6 ______________________________
____

3) -7
x +5 ______________________________
____

4) +45
x +9 ______________________________
____

5) +12
x -5 ______________________________
____

6) -26
x -14 ______________________________
____

7) -24
x -13 ______________________________
____

8) - 67
x + 8 ______________________________
____

Name ______________________________ Date ______________________________

More Multiplication With Positive and Negative Numbers

When multiplying three or more numbers, multiply from left to right. The sign of the product will be determined by the last two numbers multiplied.

Example: multiply (+8) x (-6) x (-4) = +192
Step 1: (+8) x (-6) = -48 (plus x minus = minus)
Step 2: (-48) x (-4) = +192 (minus x minus = plus)

Multiply the following problems. Place the correct sign in front of each answer. Indicate the steps followed to get the answer.

1. (-6) x (-2) x (+7) = Step 1: ____ x ____ = ____ Step 2: ____ x ____ = ____

2. (+8) x (-5) x (-9) = Step 1: ____ x ____ = ____ Step 2: ____ x ____ = ____

3. (-7) x (-8) x (-10) = Step 1: ____ x ____ = ____ Step 2: ____ x ____ = ____

4. (+7) x (+4) x (-2) = Step 1: ____ x ____ = ____ Step 2: ____ x ____ = ____

5. (-12) x (+3) x (-8) = Step 1: ____ x ____ = ____ Step 2: ____ x ____ = ____

6. (-17) x (+12) x (+3) = Step 1: ____ x ____ = ____ Step 2: ____ x ____ = ____

7. (+13) x (+3) x (+10) = Step 1: ____ x ____ = ____ Step 2: ____ x ____ = ____

8. (+4) x (-3) x (-6) x (+7) =

Step 1: ____ x ____ = ____ Step 2: ____ x ____ = ____ Step 3: ____ x ____ = ____

9. (-7) x (-6) x (-5) x (-4) =

Step 1: ____ x ____ = ____ Step 2: ____ x ____ = ____ Step 3: ____ x ____ = ____

10. (+5) x (-8) x (-3) x (+9) =

Step 1: ____ x ____ = ____ Step 2: ____ x ____ = ____ Step 3: ____ x ____ = ____

11. (-8) x (-5) x (-9) x (+3) x (-4) = Step 1: ____ x ____ = ____

Step 2: ____ x ____ = ____ Step 3: ____ x ____ = ____ Step 4: ____ x ____ = ____

12. (+21) x (-4) x (-8) x (-9) x (-10) = Step 1: ____ x ____ = ____

Step 2: ____ x ____ = ____ Step 3: ____ x ____ = ____ Step 4: ____ x ____ = ____

Name ______________________________ Date ______________________________

Division With Positive and Negative Numbers

When dividing numbers with *like* signs, find the quotient and place the positive sign in front of the quotient.

Example: $\frac{12}{6}$ = +12 ÷ +6 = +2 (dividing numbers with **like** signs)

Example: $\frac{12}{6}$ = -12 ÷ -6 = +2 (dividing numbers with **like** signs)

When dividing numbers with *unlike* signs, find the quotient and place the negative sign in front of the quotient.

Example: -$\frac{12}{6}$ = +12 ÷ -6 = -2 (dividing numbers with **unlike** signs)

Example: -$\frac{12}{6}$ = -12 ÷ +6 = -2 (dividing numbers with **unlike** signs)

Solve the following division problems using positive and negative numbers. Refer to the examples and fill in the blanks. Place the correct sign before the quotient. Write the rule for determining the sign of the quotient on the blank below each problem.

1) +$\frac{18}{3}$ = ____ ÷ ____ = ____

____

____

2) -$\frac{18}{3}$ = ____ ÷ ____ = ____

____

____

3) +$\frac{18}{3}$ = ____ ÷ ____ = ____

____

____

4) -$\frac{18}{3}$ = ____ ÷ ____ = ____

____

____

Solve the following problems. Write the quotient with the correct sign in the blank.

5) $\frac{256}{2}$ = ____

6) $\frac{625}{25}$ = ____

7) -$\frac{338}{13}$ = ____

8) $\frac{784}{14}$ = ____

Name ________________________ Date ________________________

Quiz III: Multiplication and Division with Positive and Negative Numbers

Solve the following multiplication problems using positive and negative numbers.

1. (+23) x (-14) = ____________ 2. (-13) x (-9) = ____________

3. (-123) x (+44) = ____________ 4. (+67) x (+5) x (+45) x (+12) = ____________

5. (- 34) x (+7) x (+78) = ____________ 6. (-3) x (+41) x (+2) = ____________

7. (-456) x (-12) x (-6) x (-3) = ________ 8. (+24) x (+10) x (+6) x (+2) x (-9) = ________

Solve and discover the pattern in the following multiplication problems.

9. (-2) x (-5) = ________ 10. (-6) x (-9) x (-2) = ____ 11. (-12) x (-10) x (-3) x (-5) = ____

12. (-10) x (-11) x (-9) x (-6) x (-3) = ____ 13. (-7) x (-4) x (-9) x (-10) x (-8) x (-9) = ______

14. (-2) x (-4) x (-9) x (-1) x (-7) x (-6) x (-2) = ____________________

15. (-1) x (-10) x (-11) x (-3) x (-5) x (-2) x (-1) x (-6) = ____________________

Each of the following statements has an error. Find the error and write a corrected statement on the blank below each statement.

16. When 2, 4, 6, or 8 numbers are multiplied, the product has a negative sign.

____

17. When 1, 3, 5, or 7 numbers are multiplied, the product has a positive sign.

____

Solve the following division problems using positive and negative numbers.

18. (+12) ÷ (-2) = ________ 19. (+52) ÷ (+13) = ______ 20. (-88) ÷ (-11) = ____________

21. (-125) ÷ (+5) = ______ 22. (-228) ÷ (-3) = ______ 23. (-96) ÷ (+2) = ____________

Each of the following statements contains an error. Find the error and write the correct answer on the blank below the statement.

24. When dividing two numbers with different signs, the quotient will have the sign of the larger number.

____

25. When dividing two numbers with the same sign, the quotient will have the opposite sign.

____

Name ______________________________ Date ____________________________

Mathematical Symbols

Variables

In algebra, letters are often used to represent numbers. Although any letter may be used to represent a given number, the letters x and y are used frequently. When letters are used to represent numbers, the letter may be a **constant** or a **variable**. A letter is called a variable when many different numerical values can be assigned to that letter. The variable is often called the **unknown**.

Example: $8 + x = 12$. In this case only one numerical value may be assigned to the letter x. $4, \frac{8}{2}, 3\frac{3}{3}, \frac{4}{1}$ are numerals that might replace the letter x, but the numerical value of each of the numerals is 4. In this example the letter x is a constant.

Example: $8 + x =$ ___. Any numerical value may be assigned to the letter x. In this example, the letter x is a variable. The problem can be solved by assigning any numerical value to the letter x. The number 8 is a constant because its value does not change regardless of the value assigned to x.

Equal, Less Than, Greater Than

In learning about constants and variables it is important to review some of the symbols that will be used in the lessons that follow.

A sentence with an **equals sign** (=) is an equation. An **equation** means that the number or numbers on the left of the equal sign are equal to the number or numbers on the right.

Example:

$15 = 15$
$15 = 10 + 5$
$15 = 5 + 5 + 5$
$15 = 10 + 10 - 5$
$8 + x = 12$ x must equal 4

The symbol $<$ means **less than.** If a problem states that x is less than y, then the problem is written $x < y$. You can easily remember which number is smaller because the symbol always points to the smaller number.

Example:

$14 < 15$
$13 < 10 + 5$
$12 < 5 + 5 + 4$
$11 < 8 + 8 - 3$
$8 + x < 12$ (x cannot be +4 or greater)

Name ______________________________ Date ______________________________

Equal, Less Than, Greater Than (continued)

The symbol > means **greater than.** If a problem states that *x* is greater than *y,* then the problem is written $x > y$. You can easily remember which number is smaller because the symbol always points to the smaller number.

Example:

$16 > 15$
$19 > 10 + 5$
$18 > 5 + 4 + 3$
$14 > 7 + 9 - 3$
$8 + x > 12$ (*x* must be greater than +4)

Fill in the blanks with the symbols = or < or >.

1) 3 ____ 5
2) 7 ____ 3
3) 0.3 ____ 1
4) 12 ____ 1.00
5) 1.3 ____ 1.33
6) 0.19 ____ 1.01
7) 0.22 ____ 0.022
8) 2.2 ____ 2.02
9) $\frac{1}{2}$ ____ $\frac{2}{3}$
10) $\frac{7}{2}$ ____ $\frac{2}{7}$
11) $\frac{8}{10}$ ____ 0.8
12) $\frac{10}{15}$ ____ $\frac{2}{3}$
13) $\frac{1}{2}$ ____ $\frac{2}{1}$
14) $\frac{2}{3}$ ____ $\frac{4}{6}$
15) $\frac{1}{3}$ ____ $\frac{7}{8}$
16) $\frac{7}{10}$ ____ $\frac{88}{100}$
17) $\frac{6}{10}$ ____ $\frac{3}{4}$
18) $\frac{1}{2}$ ____ $\frac{1}{3}$
19) $\frac{1}{3}$ ____ $\frac{3}{10}$
20) $\frac{5}{8}$ ____ $\frac{4}{5}$
21) $\frac{1}{9}$ ____ 0.9
22) $\frac{1}{3}$ ____ 0.33
23) $2\frac{2}{3}$ ____ 2.57
24) $3\frac{2}{5}$ ____ 3.4
25) 0.067 ____ 0.67

Name ______________________ Date ______________________

More Mathematical Symbols

Here are other mathematical symbols you will be using in algebra. You are already familiar with some of them.

($\leq$) means "is less than or equal to" $8 + x \leq 12$ x must be +4 or less
($\geq$) means "is greater than or equal to" $8 + x \geq 12$ x must be +4 or more
(+) means "to find the sum" $8 + x = 12$
(-) means "to subtract or find the difference" $8 - x = 6$
($\div$ or /) means "to divide" $8 \div x = 4$ or $8/x = 4$
(• or a number or variable written next to another number or variable) means "to multiply or find the product" $8 \bullet x = 16$ or $8x = 16$

a) Solve the following problems, and b) circle the correct word and complete the blank.

1) $16 + x = 4$ a) $x =$ _____ b) x is a (constant/variable) because ______________

____

2) $36 - 7 = y$ a) $y =$ _____ b) y a (constant/variable) because ______________

____

3) $88 \div x = 8$ a) $x =$ _____ b) x is a (constant/variable) because ______________

____

4) $12 \bullet 4 = y$ a) $y =$ _____ b) y is a (constant/variable) because ______________

____

5) $20x = 80$ a) $x =$ _____ b) x is a (constant/variable) because ______________

____

6) $144 \div 12 = b$ a) $b =$ _____ b) b is a (constant/variable) because ______________

____

7) $89 + 16 = z$ a) $z =$ _____ b) z is a (constant/variable) because ______________

____

8) $69 - x = 56$ a) $x =$ _____ b) x is a (constant/variable) because ______________

____

In the following problems you are to choose one of the numbers 0, 1, 2, 3, 4, 5, 6, 7, 8, or 9 as the numerical value for the letter in each problem. Place the number chosen in the blank following b). Solve the problem in blank a), and then circle the correct word and fill in the blank for c).

9) $16 + x =$ a)____ b) $x =$ ____ c) x is a (constant/variable) because ______________

____

Name ______________________ Date ______________________

More Mathematical Symbols (continued)

10) $36 - y =$ a) b) $y =$ _____ c) y is a (constant/variable) because ______________

____

11) $88 \div x =$ a) b) $x =$ _____ c) x is a (constant/variable) because ______________

____

12) $12 \bullet y =$ a) b) $y =$ _____ c) y is a (constant/variable) because ______________

____

13) $20x =$ a) b) $x =$ _____ c) x is a (constant/ variable) because ______________

____

14) $144 \div b =$ a) b) $b =$ _____ c) b is a (constant/variable) because ______________

____

15) $89 + z =$ a) b) $z =$ _____ c) z is a (constant/variable) because ______________

____

16) $69 - x =$ a) b) $x =$ _____ c) x is a (constant/variable) because ______________

____

Solve the following problems. Use numbers -6, -5, -4, -3, -2, -1, 0, +1, +2, +3, +4, +5, +6 in determining the answer(s) to each problem. Write the possible answers on the blank.

17a) $14 + y =$ ______________________________

b) The letter y is a (constant/variable) because ______________________

____

18a) $90 - x =$ ______________________________

b)The letter x is a (constant/variable) because ______________________

____

19a) $21 \div y > 0$ ______________________________

b)The letter y is a (constant/variable) because ______________________

____

20a) $78 + x \geq 80$ ______________________________

b)The letter x is a (constant/variable) because ______________________

____

Name ______________________ Date ______________________

Math Problems With More Than One Variable

Problems often include more than one letter or variable.

Example: $x + y = 4$

In this problem the letters x and y are both variables. Some of the numerical values that can replace x or y in the problem are 2, 1, 3, 0, 4, $3\frac{1}{2}$, $\frac{1}{2}$, and so forth. The numerical values chosen must equal 4. If $x = 4$ then y must equal 0. If $x = \frac{1}{2}$ then y must equal $3\frac{1}{2}$.

Solve the following: Choose the answers from the following numbers.

-8, -7, -6, -5, -4, -3, -2, -1, 0, +1, +2, +3, +4, +5, +6, +7, +8

Write the answers on the blank following each problem.

1) $x + y = 6$ ______________ 2) $x \div y = 36$ ______________

3) $\frac{x}{y} = 36$ ______________ 4) $xy = 25$ ______________

5) $x \bullet y = 25$ ______________ 6) $x - y = 3$ ______________

There are times when numbers and letters occur in various combinations such as those in the following examples.

$3x$, $3x - 1$, $x + 4y$, $\frac{x}{6}$, $\frac{x}{8} + 2y$, and so forth

Example: $3x =$ ___ In this expression the operation to be performed is multiplication. The 3 is a **constant** and the x is the **variable** or **unknown**. The expression indicates that 3 is to be multiplied times the value assigned to x.

Possible answers: $3 \bullet 1 = 3$; $3 \bullet 2 = 6$; $3 \bullet 3 = 9$; $3 \bullet (-1) = -3$; $3 \bullet (-2) = -6$; $3 \bullet (-3) = -9$

Solve the following problems.

7) If $x = 5$ then $4x =$ _____ 8) If $x = 7$ then $4 \bullet x =$ ____ 9) If $x = -7$ then $4x =$ _____

10) If $y = 5$ then $3y - 1 =$ ____ 11) If $y = 6$ then $3y - 1 =$ ____ 12) If $y = -2$ then $3y - 1 =$ ____

13) If $t = 36$ then $\frac{t}{6} =$ _____ 14) If $t = -18$ then $\frac{t}{6} =$ _____ 15) If $t = -48$ then $t \div 6 =$ ____

16) If $x = 24$ and $y = 4$ then $\frac{x}{8} + 2y =$ ____ 17) If $x = -144$ and $y = -5$ then $\frac{x}{8} + 2y =$ _____

18) If $x = -9$ and $y = -3$ then $x + 4y =$ ____ 19) If $x = 46$ and $y = -12$ then $x + 4y =$ _____

20) If $b = 4$ and $t = 7$ then $bt - tb =$ _____

Name ______________________________ Date ______________________________

Word Problems Using Variables

Solve the following problems.

1) Emily and two friends wanted to buy a pizza. A small pizza cost $4.50. The next larger pizza cost one dollar more than twice as much as the $4.50 one. They decided to buy the larger pizza. One of them said the algebraic expression to determine the cost could be written as $2x + 1$.

The numeral "2" in the expression is used to mean:

a) twice as much b) $4.50 c) one dollar.

2) In solving the problem, the letter "x" in the expression will be replaced by:

a) $1 b) $4.50 c) 2

3) Place the correct numbers in the expression and find the cost of the pizza.

2 • ____ + 1 = $ _____

4) Another evening Emily and two friends wanted to buy a pizza. They called another pizza shop and were told that a small pizza cost $4.50. The next larger pizza cost one dollar less than twice as much as the $4.50 one. They decided to buy the larger pizza. The bill was $8.00.

Complete each of the following algebraic expressions and determine which one would give Emily and her friends the correct answer.

a) $2x + 1$ = 2 • _____ + 1 = _____ b) $3x + 1$ = 3 • _____ + 1 = _____

c) $3x - 1$ = 3 • _____ -1 = _____ d) $2x - 1$ = 2 • _____ -1 = _____

5) The algebraic expression that gives the correct answer to the cost of the pizza is

_____ - _____ = $8.00

6) The algebraic expression tells you to take ____ times $____ and (add/subtract) $ ____

7) In the blank following each algebraic expression write out in your own words what the expression tells you to do.

a) xy ______________________________

b) $\frac{x}{y}$ ______________________________

c) $x + y$ ______________________________

d) $x - y$ ______________________________

e) $\frac{x}{y} + ts - 2$ ______________________________

f) $x + \frac{y}{3} + 1$ ______________________________

g) $x \bullet y$ ______________________________

Name ______________________________ Date ___________________________

Quiz IV: Mathematical Symbols

Match the correct definition in Column B with the term or symbol in Column A.

	Column A	Column B
_____	1) Variable	A) Symbol meaning "to divide"
_____	2) Constant	B) Symbol meaning "equal to"
_____	3) $=$	C) Symbol meaning "greater than"
_____	4) $\neq$	D) Symbol meaning "does not equal"
_____	5) $\div$	E) Symbol meaning "to find the sum"
_____	6) $>$	F) Symbol meaning "equal to or greater than"
_____	7) $<$	G) Symbol meaning "to find the difference"
_____	8) $\geq$	H) Letter in algebraic expression that may have different values
_____	9) $\leq$	I) Variables are to be multiplied
_____	10) $-$	J) A number stated in the algebraic expression
_____	11) $+$	K) Symbol meaning "equal to or less than"
_____	12) xy	L) Symbol meaning "less than"

Write a statement explaining what each of the following algebraic expressions directs you to do.

13) $x = y + 1$ ____

14) $5 \geq x$ ____

15) $\frac{t}{w} - cu$ ____

16) $x + 1 < 5$ ____

17) $x \neq y$ ____

18) $6 + 7 > x$ ____

Name ______________________________ Date ______________________________

Understanding Polynomials

Definitions

A **polynomial** is an algebraic expression of two or more terms. In learning about polynomials it is important to understand the meaning of the words **number, variable, product, quotient, sum, difference, term,** and **expression.**

- **Number:** You have already learned about the Real Numbers. Real Numbers include the positive and negative numbers ...-5, -4, -3, -2, -1, 0, 1, 2, 3, 4, 5... and numbers that can be expressed as fractions ($\frac{a}{b}$) ...$-\frac{1}{4}$, $-\frac{1}{2}$, $-1\frac{1}{2}$, $-1\frac{2}{3}$, $\frac{1}{4}$, $\frac{1}{2}$, $\frac{2}{3}$, $\frac{5}{8}$, $2\frac{3}{4}$, $23\frac{2}{3}$...
- **Variable:** A symbol that may be replaced by one or more numbers. Usually letters of the alphabet are used as variables. In algebra *x* and *y* are often used. A variable may appear alone as *x* or with some other letter. Often the variable will appear with a number. For example, the number 2 with the variable *x* becomes 2*x* or 2 multiplied by *x*. In this case *x* is a variable because any number may be substituted for the variable *x*.
- **Product:** The result of multiplication. For example, in 3 • 6 = 18, 18 is the product.
- **Quotient:** The result of division. For example, in $\frac{6}{3}$ = 2, 2 is the quotient.
- **Sum:** The result of addition. For example, in 6 + 3 = 9, 9 is the sum.
- **Difference:** The result of subtraction. For example, in 6 - 2 = 4, 4 is the difference.
- **Term:** Parts of an expression separated by plus or minus signs. For example: 4*x* - 7*y* is a mathematical expression. Both 4*x* and 7*y* are terms.
- **Expression:** A combination of letters and numbers joined by plus symbols, minus symbols, multiplication symbols, or division symbols.

Place a plus (+) on the blanks before the items below that are **numbers**.

_1) *x* _2) 8 _3) 321 _4) *xy* _5) $\frac{3}{4}$ _6) $56\frac{2}{5}$ _7) 24

Place a plus (+) on the blanks before the items below that are **variables**.

_8) *y* _9) $6\frac{1}{2}$ _10) *xy* _11) $\frac{7}{8}$ _12) $\frac{x}{y}$ _13) 567 _14) *b*

Place a plus (+) on the blanks before the problems below where a **product** would result.

_15) 6 • 7 _16) 5 • *x* _17) 8 + 3 _18) $5\frac{6}{3}$ _19) 12 • 45 _20) 6 • *x* • y

Place a plus (+) on the blanks before the problems below where a **quotient** would result.

_21) $\frac{2}{3} \cdot \frac{1}{2}$ _22) $4\frac{5}{9}$ _23) $\frac{a}{b}$ _24) *x* + *y* _25) *xy* _26) $\frac{\frac{1}{2}}{\frac{2}{3}}$ _27) -10 + 5

Place a plus (+) on the blanks before the problems below where a **sum** would result.

_28) 23 + 78 _29) $\frac{3}{4} + \frac{1}{2}$ _30) $23\frac{2}{3} + 21\frac{3}{4}$ _31) 45*x* _32) $2\frac{4}{6}$ _33) 7 - 4

Place a plus (+) on the blanks before the problems below where a **difference** would result.

_34) *x* - b _35) *x* + b _36) 56 - 31 _37) $\frac{66}{11}$ _38) $\frac{x}{b}$ _39) $3\frac{1}{2} - 2\frac{1}{3}$ _40) 72 - (-8)

Name ______________________ Date ______________________

Terms, Expressions, and Polynomials

A **term** is an expression that may be a number and a variable, a number, a variable, or the product or quotient of numbers and/or variables. **A term represents one number.**

For example: 5, $5a$, $5ab$, $5a^2b$, $5a^2b^2$, $\frac{4}{2}$ are all terms that represent one number.
For each term in the example above let $a = 2$, $b = 3$, and find what number each of the terms represents.

$5 = 5$; $5a = 5 \bullet 2 = 10$; $5ab = 5 \bullet 2 \bullet 3 = 30$; $5a^2b = 5 \bullet 2^2 \bullet 3 = 60$;
$5a^2b^2 = 5 \bullet 2^2 \bullet 3^2 = 180$; $\frac{4}{2} = 2$

Each of the above terms represents one number.

Place a plus (+) on the blanks before the items below that are **terms**.

_ 1) $3a$ _ 2) 34 _ 3) y _ 4) $21 + 6$ _ 5) $89 - 23$ _ 6) $8ax$ _ 7) $x + y$

_ 8) $3x - y$ _ 9) $3/b$ _ 10) $x + y/5$ _ 11) $9sn$

In algebra the word **expression** is used frequently. An **expression** consists of one, two, or three terms and represents a **number**. In an expression, the terms are composed of **numbers** and **letters (variables)** together or **numbers** and **letters (variables)** separately. For example: The expression $5a$ has one term. The expression 5 has one term. The expression $5a + 5$ has two terms. The expression $5a - 2b + 5$ has three terms.

When an expression includes terms using both numbers and letters (variables), the expression is called an *algebraic expression*.

Place a plus (+) on the blanks before the expressions below that have **two or more terms**.

_ 12) xy _ 13) $x + y$ _ 14) $x - y$ _ 15) $6a - b$ _ 16) $8x + \frac{7}{8}$ _ 17) $2xy/2$

_ 18) $5z - 2x$ _ 19) $32 + xy$ _ 20) $9x$ _ 21) $4xy$ _ 22) s/b _ 23) $s/x + 10a$

Polynomial refers to an **expression** of one, two, or three **terms**. Polynomials of one term are called **monomials**. Polynomials of two terms are called **binomials**. Polynomials of three terms are called **trinomials**.

All of the following are polynomial expressions. Place the letter "M" before the monomials. Place the letter "B" before the binomials. Place the letter "T" before the trinomials.

_ 24) $6y$ _ 25) $6y + x$ _ 26) $6y - 2$ _ 27) $x + y + a/b$ _ 28) $3b - 2a + 6$ _ 29) x/b

_ 30) $\frac{2}{3}x$ _ 31) $\frac{2}{3}x - 6a$ _ 32) x _ 33) $\frac{1}{3}x + \frac{2}{3}y - 8$ _ 34) $xt + 7/n$ _ 35) $10xb^2$

Name ______________________ Date ______________________

Adding Polynomials

Like Terms

Algebra problems often require adding, subtracting, multiplying, and dividing polynomials.

When adding polynomials *like terms* are added. Like terms have the same variable and the same exponent.

For example, in the list of terms: $2x^2$, x^2, $10x^2$, $-3x^3$, the first three terms are like terms because they have the same variable and the same exponent. These three may be added together, but $-3x^3$ cannot because the exponent is different, and therefore it is not a like term.

Example 1:

In the polynomial $x^3 + x^2 + 3x^3 + x^2$ the like terms can be added. Adding the like terms $x^3 + 3x^3 = 4x^3$ and $x^2 + x^2 = 2x^2$.

So like terms are added and $x^3 + x^2 + 3x^3 + x^2$ becomes $4x^3 + 2x^2$, a simplified form of the original polynomial.

Example 2:

Add $-x^4 + 3y^2 - x^2$ and $3x^4 - 4x^2 + 2y^2$.

One way to add polynomials is to select one of the variables and arrange the like terms in descending power. In this example the variable x is selected as the variable to use in arranging the like terms in descending power.

So: $-x^4 + 3y^2 - x^2$ becomes $-x^4 - x^2 + 3y^2$ plus $3x^4 - 4x^2 + 2y^2$, which becomes $3x^4 - 4x^2 + 2y^2$

Adding like terms $-x^4 + 3y^2 - x^2$ plus $3x^4 - 4x^2 + 2y^2$

Simplified = $2x^4 - 5x^2 + 5y^2$

Example 3:

Add $(-2x^2 + 2x - y^2) - (x^2 + x - y)$. When adding these polynomials, the parentheses must be removed. Refer to Learning About Parentheses and Brackets on page 40 for a further discussion of working with parentheses and brackets. $(-2x^2 + 2x - y^2)$ is assumed to have a positive (+) sign in front of the parentheses, so the parentheses can be removed without changing the signs inside the parentheses.

In the case of $-(x^2 + x - y)$ the parentheses are preceded by a negative (-) sign. In this case, each sign inside the parentheses must be changed when the parentheses are removed. $-(x^2 + x - y)$ is rewritten without the parentheses as $-x^2 - x + y$.

Now the polynomial reads: $-2x^2 + 2x - y^2 - x^2 - x + y$, and you can add like terms. The complete problem is shown below.

$(-2x^2 + 2x - y^2) - (x^2 + x - y) = -2x^2 + 2x - y^2 - x^2 - x + y = -3x^2 + x - y^2 + y$ (simplified).

Name ________________________ Date ________________________

Adding Polynomials (continued)

Circle the terms in each group that can be added.

1) $2x^2$ x^3 x^2 y^3 $3x$

2) $7x^3$ n^5 t^3 x^3 $7x$

3) y^4 $3y^4$ $2xy$ y x^5

4) p^2 p^4 $6x^2$ t^2 $2p^4$

5) t^4 rt^2 $3t^4$ y^3 $10t^4$

6) s^3 $12s^2$ $4x$ $2x$ s

7) $8y^3$ $5y^3$ y^3 x^3 $2x^3$

8) k $3k$ t^3 $6k$ $5t^2$

9) y^2 x^2 $2x$ $3y$ t^3

10) x^4 $10x^2$ $8x^5$ $2x^2$ x^2

Simplify the following by adding like terms.

11) $2x + 3x - 4x =$ ____________

12) $10y - 4y =$ ____________

13) $(5x) - (2x) =$ ____________

14) $(5x) - (-2x) =$ ____________

15) $3x^2 - 2x + y^2 + x^2 - x + y^2 =$ ____________________

16) $-5y^2 + 3x^2 + 2y^2 - x^2 =$ ____________________

17) $-(-5y^2 + 3x^2) + (-2y^2 - x^2) =$ ________________________________

18) $3x^4 - 2x^3 + x^2 - y^2 + y - 2y^2 + x^3 + y - x^4 + 3y^2 =$ ____________________

____

19) $-(-3x^4 + 2x^3 - x^2 + y^2 - y) - (2y^2 - x^3 - y + x^4 - 3y^2) =$ ____________________

____

20) $-(-x^2 + y^2 - 3y^3 + x^4) + (-x^3 + y^2 - 2y^3 - 4x^4) =$ ____________________

____

Name ______________________ Date ______________________

Subtracting Polynomials

When subtracting polynomials, they are arranged in column form and like terms are subtracted.

Remember to arrange the polynomials so that like terms will appear in each column.

Example 1 : Subtract $3x - 2y$ from $5x + y$

Step 1: Arrange the polynomials in column form with like terms in the same column.

$$\begin{array}{rl} & 5x + y \\ - & \underline{3x - 2y} \text{ subtrahend} \end{array}$$

Step 2: Change the sign of the terms in the subtrahend. Now add the columns.

$$\begin{array}{rl} & 5x + y \\ + & \underline{-3x + 2y} \text{ subtrahend} \\ & 2x + 3y \end{array}$$

Example 2: Subtract $(3x^2 - y^2 + z) - (x^2 - y^2 - 2z)$

Step1: Remove the parentheses. Remember to change the sign inside the parentheses when the parentheses are preceded by a negative (-) sign.

$$(3x^2 - y^2 + z) - (x^2 - y^2 - 2z) = 3x^2 - y^2 + z - x^2 + y^2 + 2z$$

Step 2: Arrange the like terms in column form, and add.

$$\begin{array}{rl} & 3x^2 - y^2 + z \\ - & \underline{+x^2 - y^2 - 2z} \end{array} \qquad \begin{array}{rl} & 3x^2 - y^2 + z \\ + & \underline{-x^2 + y^2 + 2z} \\ & 2x^2 \qquad + 3z \end{array}$$

Subtract the following polynomials. Arrange in column form. Remember to change the sign of the subtrahend and add.

1) $(2xy - 3x + 4y) - (xy + x - 27) =$

2) $-(4x - 3b) - (x + 2b) =$

3) $(3x^3 - 2x^2 - x + y) - (2x^3 + x^2 + x - y) =$

4) $(5x + 4y - 2a) - (4x + a) =$

5) $(12x^3 + 10y^2 + y) - (x - y^2 - y) =$

6) $(12x^3 + 10y^2 + y) - (x^3 - y^2 - y) =$

7) $-(12x^3 + 10y^2 + y) - (x^3 - y^2 - y) =$

8) $-(12x^3 + 10y^2 + y) + (x^3 - y^2 - y) =$

Name ______________________ Date ______________________

Multiplying Polynomials

When multiplying a polynomial by a *monomial*, each term of the polynomial is multiplied by the monomial. For example, $2(x + y) = 2x + 2y$. When the monomial 2 is multiplied by each term of the polynomial $(x + y)$ the result is $2x + 2y$.

In reviewing exponents note that: $x^1 = x$; $x^2 = x \bullet x$; $x^3 = x \bullet x \bullet x$; $x^4 = x \bullet x \bullet x \bullet x$; etc.

In learning to multiply polynomials it is important to review the multiplication of exponents.
Example 1:

Multiply: $x^1 \bullet x^1 = x^{1+1} = x^2$ $y^2 \bullet y^3 = y^{2+3} = y^5$

Multiply: $2x^1 \bullet 3x^1 = 6x^{1+1} = 6x^2$ $3y^2 \bullet 4y^3 = 12y^{2+3} = 12y^5$

Example 2: Multiply $(x + y)$ times $2 = 2(x + y) = 2x + 2y$

Multiply $(x^2 + y^2)$ times $2x = 2x(x^2 + y^2) = 2x^{1+2} + 2xy^2 = 2x^3 + 2xy^2$

Note: In multiplying the polynomials, the numbers preceding the variables are multiplied as usual. To multiply like variables, add the exponents.

Multiply the following

1) $3(x - y) =$ ______ - ______

2) $3x(x + y) =$ ______ + ______

3) $t^2(t^3 - y^2) =$ ______ - ______

4) $-2x(x^2 + x - y) =$ ______________________

5) $-3y^2(-3xy) =$ ______________________

6) $5x(-3x^3 + 2x^2 - xy + y) =$ ______________________

7) $-5x(-3x^3 + 2x^2 - xy + y) =$ ______________________

8) $-3xy(14xy^2) =$ ______________________

9) $-3x^2y(-14xy^2) =$ ______________________

10) $3a^2(2a^3 - 3a^3) =$ ______________________

Name ______________________ Date ______________________

Multiplying Polynomials (continued)

In all of the problems on the previous page, a monomial was multiplied by a polynomial. However, many times a polynomial is multiplied by a polynomial.

Example 3:

When multiplying a polynomial by a polynomial, arrange the polynomials in column form. Find the product of $(2x - y)(x + y)$. Note the steps in multiplying polynomials.

Multiplying from left to right

Step 1: Multiply x times $2x$
Step 2: Multiply x times $-y$
Step 3: Multiply y times $2x$
Step 4: Multiply y times $-y$

Steps 1 & 2

$$\begin{array}{r} 2x - y \\ \bullet \quad x \\ \hline 2x^2 - xy \end{array}$$

Steps 3 & 4

$$\begin{array}{r} 2x - y \\ \bullet \quad y \\ \hline 2xy - y^2 \end{array}$$

Step 5: Add the partial products: $2x^2 - xy + 2xy - y^2 = 2x^2 + xy - y^2$

Multiply the following and simplify:

11) $(3x - 2y)(x + y)$

$$\begin{array}{r} 3x - 2y \\ \bullet \quad x \\ \hline \end{array} \qquad \begin{array}{r} 3x - 2y \\ \bullet \quad y \\ \hline \end{array}$$

Add partial products: ______________

12) $(x^2 + 1)(x - y)$

____

13) $(-3x^2 + y^3)(x^2 - y^2)$

____

14) $(x - y)(-x - y)$

____

15) $(-x - y^3)(-x + y)$

____

16) $(t - x^4)(2t - x^4)$

____

Name ______________________ Date ______________________

Dividing Polynomials

When dividing polynomials, the division of like variables becomes very important.

Example 1: To divide like variables x^4/x^2 the exponents are subtracted.

Step 1: Subtract the exponents: 4 - 2 = 2

Step 2: Rewrite the variable with the exponent 2

$x^4/x^2 = x^{4-2} = x^2$

Example 2: Divide x^2/x^4

Step1: Subtract the exponents: 2 - 4 = -2

Step 2: Rewrite the variable with the exponent -2

$x^2/x^4 = x^{2-4} = x^{-2}$

Step 3: Rewrite x^{-2} as the denominator of a fraction with a numerator 1.

$1/x^2$

Example 3: Divide $9x^3y/3xy$

Step 1: Rewrite as $\frac{9x^3y}{3xy}$

Step 2: Divide 9 by 3 = $\frac{3x^3y}{xy}$

Step 3: Subtract the exponents of like variables

$x^{3-1} = x^2$ and $y^{1-1} = y^0 = 1$

Step 4: Rewrite the problem

$3x^2$ ($y^0 = 1$: When the variable is 1 it is not rewritten.)

Example 4: Divide $9xy/3x^3y$

Step 1: Rewrite as $\frac{9xy}{3x^3y}$

Step 2: Divide 9 by 3 = $\frac{3xy}{x^3y}$

Step 3: Subtract the exponents of like variables

$x^{1-3} = x^{-2} = 1/x^2$ and $y^{1-1} = y^0 = 1$

Step 4: Rewrite the problem

$3 \bullet 1/x^2$ or $\frac{3}{x^2}$ ($y^0 = 1$: When the variable is 1, it is not rewritten.)

Solve the following

1) $x^5/x^3 =$ ______________________

2) $y^8/y^4 =$ ______________________

3) $t^2/t =$ ______________________

4) $4x^3/2x =$ ______________________

5) $12y^4/3y^3 =$ ______________________

6) $x^3/x =$ ______________________

7) $x^3/x^5 =$ ______________________

8) $y^4/y^8 =$ ______________________

9) $t/t^2 =$ ______________________

10) $-4x^3/2x =$ ______________________

11) $12y^4/-3y^3 =$ ______________________

12) $-x^3/-x =$ ______________________

Name ______________________________ Date ______________________________

Dividing Polynomials (continued)

When dividing a polynomial by a monomial, divide each term of the polynomial by the monomial.

Example 5: Divide $(rt + st)/t = \frac{rt + st}{t} = \frac{1(r\not{t})}{\not{t}} + \frac{1(s\not{t})}{\not{t}} = r + s$

The polynomial is $rt + st$. Each term rt and st must be divided by the monomial t.

Example 6: Divide $(6x^2y + 4x^3)/2xy = \frac{6x^2y}{2xy} + \frac{4x^3}{2xy} = \frac{\overset{3x^1y^0}{\not{6x^2y}}}{\not{2xy}} + \frac{\overset{2x^2}{\not{4x^3}}}{\not{2x}y} = \frac{3x + 2x^2}{y}$

Divide the following and simplify.

13) $(14x^4 + 6x^3)/2x =$ a) $\frac{14x^4}{2x} + \frac{6x^3}{2x} =$ b) ____ + ____

14) $(3y^2 - 3y)/3y =$ a) ____ - ____ = b) ____ - ____

15) $(9r^6 - 12r^3 + 6r)/3r^2 =$ a) ____ - ____ + ____ = b) ____ - ____ + ____

16) $(14x^4 + 6x^3)/-2x =$ a) ____ + ____ = b) ____ + ____

17) $(3y^2 - 3x)/-3y =$ a) ____ - ____ = b) ____ - ____

18) $(-14x^4 + 6x^3)/2x =$ a) ____ + ____ = b) ____ + ____

19) $(ab + as)/a =$ a) ____ + ____ = b) ____ + ____

20) $(10c - 5a)/5 =$ a) ____ - ____ = b) ____ - ____

Name ______________________________ Date ______________________________

Quiz V: Understanding Polynomials

Match the definition in Column B with its corresponding term in Column A by placing the letter next to the term.

	Column A	Column B
_____	1) Variable	A) Result of the multiplication process
_____	2) Term	B) Result of the addition process
_____	3) Product	C) Result of the division process
_____	4) Quotient	D) Letter used to represent numbers
_____	5) Sum	E) Result of the subtraction process
_____	6) Difference	F) An expression referring to a number, variable, or number and variable representing one number
_____	7) Monomial	G) An algebraic expression of one or more terms
_____	8) Polynomial	H) A polynomial with one term
_____	9) Binomial	I) A polynomial with two terms
_____	10) Trinomial	J) A polynomial with three terms

Circle the like terms in the following list

11) $3x^3$ x^2 $5x^2$ y $3y^3$

Simplify the following (add or combine).

12) $5y + 10y + 2y^2 - y^2 =$ ______________________________

13) $-(2x^2 - 3x + 5y) + (10x^2 + 4x - 6y) =$ ______________________________

Simplify the following (subtract). To solve, arrange in column form in space to right of problem.

14) $-2y^2 + 5y$ from $6y^2 - 2y$

Simplified =

15) $-7x^3 - 6y^3 + 4y^2 - 3$ from $10x^3 - 3y^3 - 2y^2 + 2 =$

Simplified =

Name ______________________________ Date ______________________________

Quiz V: Understanding Polynomials (continued)

Simplify the following (multiply). To solve, arrange in column form in space to right of problem and show all work.

16) $(2x^2 + y)(3x^3 - 2y)$

Simplified =

17) $-(x^3 + 2x^2) \bullet -(x^3 - x^2)$

Simplified =

Simplify the following (divide). Show all work in space to right of problem.

18) $6y^4/2y^2$

Simplified =

19) $-6y^2 /2y^4$

Simplified =

20) $(8y^4 - 4y^3 - 2y^2)/2y$

Simplified =

Name ______________________ Date ______________________

Learning About Equations

Written and Mathematical Expressions

An *equation* is a mathematical statement of equality in which two numbers or algebraic expressions are said to be equal. Equations are important in the study of algebra since they are the primary method of solving problems. Understanding equations is not difficult. Every day we use mathematical expressions and easily understand them. Some of the English expressions we use and their mathematical counterparts are listed below.

English Expression	Mathematical Expression
Five more than a number	$y + 5$
Five added to a number	$y + 5$
A number is increased by five	$y + 5$
Five less than a number	$y - 5$
Five subtracted from a number	$y - 5$
A number is decreased by five	$y - 5$
Five more than two times a number	$2y + 5$
Five added to two times a number	$2y + 5$
Five less than two times a number	$2y - 5$
Five subtracted from two times a number	$2y - 5$
Five times a number	$5y$
One-fifth of a number	$y \div 5$ or y/5

Read the following written expressions and rewrite them as mathematical expressions. Use the letter *y* to represent the unknown number.

1) Seven more than a specific number ______________________
2) Three less than a specific number ______________________
3) Ten added to a specific number ______________________
4) Thirteen subtracted from a specific number ______________________
5) A specific number decreased by seven ______________________
6) Eight times a specific number ______________________
7) Three more than five times a specific number ______________________
8) Nine times a specific number ______________________
9) Five more than three times a specific number ______________________
10) Sixteen less than two times a specific number ______________________
11) A specific number increased by 40 ______________________
12) One-fifth more than a specific number ______________________
13) Two-thirds less than a specific number ______________________
14) Six less than one-tenth of a specific number ______________________
15) Five more than one-eighth of a specific number ______________________

Name ______________________ Date ______________________

Written and Mathematical Expressions (continued)

Change the following sentences into mathematical equations.

16) A number multiplied by five, plus six is equal to 50. ______________
17) A number divided by five, less seven is equal to 37. ______________
18) A number plus 17, plus three, minus 12 equals 15. ______________
19) If you subtract 8 from a specific number you get 12. ______________
20) If you multiply a number by 13 you get 117. ______________
21) Alonzo bought 5 boxes of trading cards. There were the same number in each box. He bought a total of 55 trading cards. ______________
22) If you add six to five times a number, your answer will be 45 more than twice the number. ______________
23) Three times a certain number is the same as that number plus 15. ______________
24) Seventeen more than twice a number is 48. ______________
25) Take a number, double it, add 7 and you get 23. ______________
26) If you add $\frac{1}{3}$ to 7 times a certain number you get 100. ______________
27) If you add 13 to seven times a number, your answer is 127 more than the number itself. ______________
28) Bill ate three slices of pizza. Jim ate three times as many. Jim consumed 1,000 calories. How many calories did Bill consume? ______________
29) Juanita can jog twice as far today as she could a year ago. A year ago she could jog one and a half miles. How far can she jog today? ______________
30) Mary scored a certain number of points. Emily scored one less than twice as many. Emily scored thirty points. How many points did Mary score? ______________

Here are some well-known mathematical expressions. Write them as equations.

31) The perimeter of rectangle (P) is equal to twice its width (W) added to twice its length (L). ______________
32) The area (a) of a rectangle is equal to the product of the length (L) and the width (W). ______________
33) The area of a triangle is equal to $\frac{1}{2}$ the product of the base (b) and the height (h). ______________
34) The area of a circle is *pi* (π) times the radius (r) squared. ______________
35) Centigrade temperature (C) can be found by taking the Fahrenheit temperature (F) less 32°, and multiplying it by $\frac{5}{9}$. ______________

Name ______________________________ Date ______________________________

Equations

You have learned that polynomials like $3 + x$, $x + y$, or $6y$ are called algebraic expressions. In **algebraic expressions** any numbers can be substituted for the variables x and y.

An **equation** is a mathematical statement of equality. It states that two numbers or algebraic expressions are equal. The algebraic expressions $3 + x$, $x + y$, and $6y$ are written below as parts of equations.

$$3 + x = 7 \quad x + y = 20 \quad 6y = 42$$

In each case the algebraic expressions have been connected to another expression by an equal sign. Connect the expressions with an equal (=) sign and you have a mathematical statement of equality or an equation.

In solving equations it is important to emphasize the equal sign. In solving the equation you must find numbers that can be substituted for the variable(s) so that the two expressions are equal. **The solutions for the equation must be true.** This means that the solutions found must make the two expressions in the equation equal.

For example, in the equation $3 + x = 7$ if the number 4 is substituted for x, the two expressions are equal. The equation has been solved with a true solution. If you substitute any other whole number for the x, the two expressions are no longer equal.

Complete the following exercise. Solve the equations below so that there are true solutions to the equations.

1) $5 + y = 9$ Solution: $y =$ ______
2) $5 - x = 4$ Solution: $x =$ ______
3) $s + t = 9$ Solutions: If $s = 4$, then $t =$ ______ If $s = 1$, then $t =$ ______
4) $s - t = 6$ Solutions: If $s = 16$, then $t =$ ______ If $s = 9$, then $t =$ ______
5) $6y = 36$ Solution: $y =$ ______
6) $2x + 5 = 17$ Solution: $x =$ ______
7) $2x + r = 15$ Solutions: If $x = -3$, then $r =$ ______ If $s = 6$, then $r =$ ______
8) $2y - 2 = 12$ Solution: $y =$ ______
9) $2y - x = 12$ Solutions: If $y = 8$, then $x =$ ______ If $y = 10$, then $x =$ ______
10) $15/x = 3$ Solution: $x =$ ______

Name ______________________________ Date ____________________________

Understanding Equations

An easy way to understand equations is by visualizing a scale. If both sides of a scale have the same amount of weight, then the scale balances as in the following illustration.

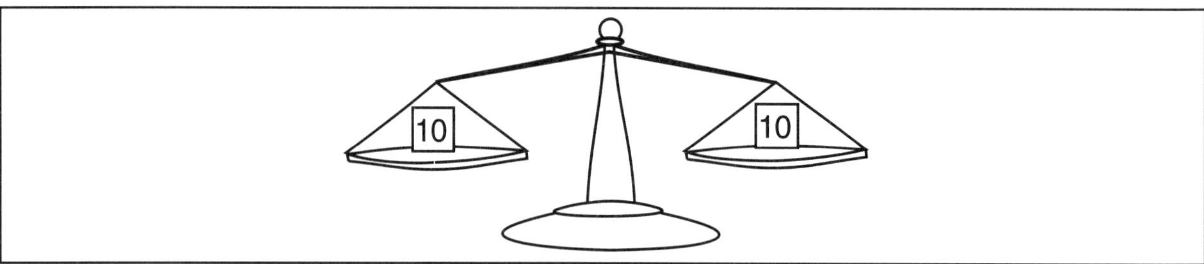

An equation can be compared to a scale because both sides of an equation are equal.

10 = 10

Both sides have ten pounds of weight, so the scale is perfectly balanced. It really doesn't matter if the weights on both sides of the scale are each ten-pound blocks or a combination of weights that total ten pounds. If the weight on each side of the scale is equal to the other, then the scale balances as it does in the following illustrations.

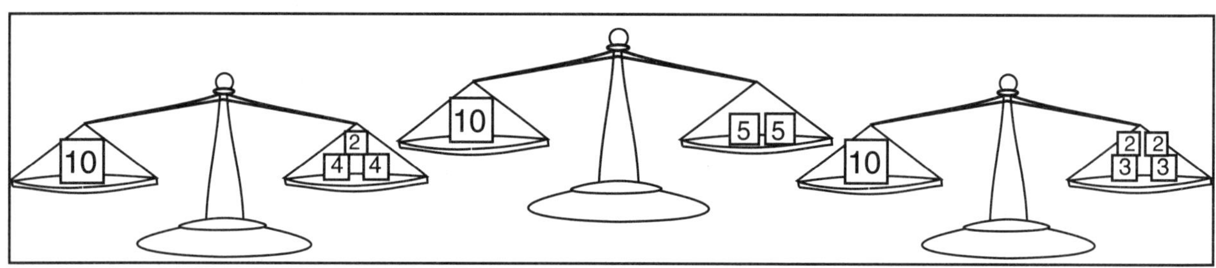

Similarly, an equation is true if it is equal on both sides of the equal sign.

10 = 4 + 4 + 2 **10 = 5 + 5** **10 = 3 + 3 + 2 + 2**

If you do the same thing to both sides of a scale they remain balanced. If you do the same thing to both sides of an equation, they also remain equal.

Here are some examples using the scale.

Example:

If you have a scale with ten pounds on either side, it is perfectly balanced. If you add four pounds to each side of the scale, each side will then have 14 pounds, but the scales will remain perfectly balanced.

Name ______________________________ Date ______________________

Understanding Equations (continued)

If you **add** the same number to both sides of an equation, the equation remains true.

$$10 = 10$$
$$10 + 4 = 10 + 4$$
$$14 = 14$$

If you **remove** four pounds from each side of the scale, each side will have six pounds, and the scale will remain perfectly balanced.

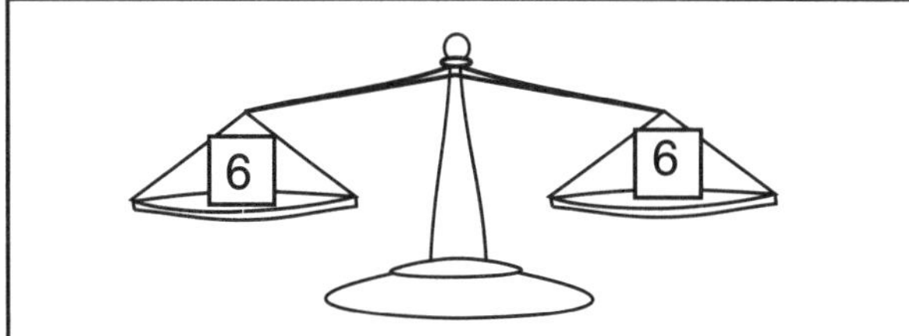

If you **subtract** the same number from both sides of an equation, the equation remains true.

$$10 = 10$$
$$10 - 4 = 10 - 4$$
$$6 = 6$$

If you **multiply** each ten-pound weight by three, each side will have thirty pounds and will remain perfectly balanced.

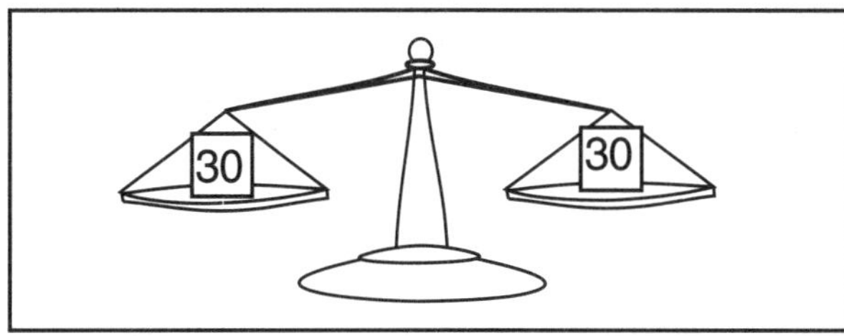

If you **multiply** both sides of an equation by the same number, the equation remains true.

$$10 = 10$$
$$10 \bullet 3 = 10 \bullet 3$$
$$30 = 30$$

If you **divide** each ten-pound weight by two, each side will have five pounds and will remain perfectly balanced.

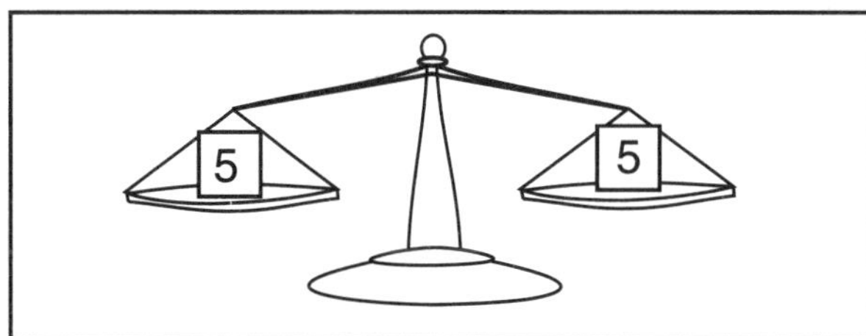

If you **divide** both sides of an **equation** by the same number, the equation remains true.

$$10 = 10$$
$$10 \div 2 = 10 \div 2$$
$$5 = 5$$

Remember, if you do the same thing to both sides of an equation, both sides remain equal and the equation remains true.

Name ______________________________ Date ____________________________

Review of Equation Rules

Here is a review of some of the rules to use when studying equations.

The same number may be added to both sides of an equation, and the equation will remain true.

Example:

Begin with the equation $y - 8 = 23$

Add +8 to each side, and the equation becomes $y - 8 + 8 = 23 + 8$

Which means $y = 31$

Transposition **is the practice of moving a quantity from one side of the equation to the other and changing its sign to the opposite sign.**

Transposition is basically what occurred in the above example. Transposition is often used to change the equation so that the unknown quantity is on one side of the equation and the known quantity on the other. Transposition is also used in the following examples. Solve the following. The first one has been completed.

1) $x - 7 = 14$ a) $x - 7 + 7 = 14 + 7$ b) $x = 21$ c) $21 - 7 = 14$

2) $x - 9 = 3$ a) ________ b) ________ c) ________

3) $x - 15 = 55$ a) ________ b) ________ c) ________

4) $x - 18 = 10$ a) ________ b) ________ c) ________

The same number may be subtracted from both sides of an equation, and the equation will remain true.

Example:

Begin with the equation $y + 8 = 23$

Subtract -8 from each side and the equation becomes $y + 8 - 8 = 23 - 8$

Which means $y = 15$

Solve the following. The first one has been completed.

5) $x + 7 = 14$ a) $x + 7 - 7 = 14 - 7$ b) $x = 7$ c) $7 + 7 = 7$

6) $x + 9 = 23$ a) ________ b) ________ c) ________

7) $x + 15 = 55$ a) ________ b) ________ c) ________

8) $x + 18 = 28$ a) ________ b) ________ c) ________

Name ______________________________ Date ______________________________

Review of Equation Rules (continued)

Each side of an equation may be multiplied by the same number, and the equation will remain true. Zero cannot be used.

Example:

Begin with the equation: $\frac{y}{6} = 72$

Multiply each side by 6 and the equation becomes: $\frac{y}{6} \bullet 6 = 72 \bullet 6$

Which means: $y = 432$

Solve the following. The first one has been completed for you.

9) $\frac{x}{8} = 2$ a) $8 \bullet \frac{x}{8} = 2 \bullet 8$ b) $x = 16$ c) Check: $\frac{16}{8} = 2$

10) $\frac{y}{9} = 3$ a) ________ b) ________ c) ________

11) $\frac{y}{2} = 32$ a) ________ b) ________ c) ________

12) $\frac{x}{25} = 125$ a) ________ b) ________ c) ________

13) $\frac{y}{4} = 15$ a) ________ b) ________ c) ________

Both sides of an equation may be divided by the same number, and the equation will remain true. Zero cannot be used.

Example:

Begin with the equation $6y = 72$

Divide each side by 6 and the equation becomes $\frac{6y}{6} = \frac{72}{6}$

Which means $y = 12$

Solve the following. The first one has been completed.

14) $5x = 25$ a) $\frac{5x}{5} = \frac{25}{5}$ b) $\frac{\cancel{5}x}{\cancel{5}} = \frac{\cancel{25}^{5}}{\cancel{5}}$ c) $x = 5$ d) check $5 \bullet 5 = 25$

15) $9y = 576$ a) b) c) ________ d) ________

16) $12x = 12$ a) b) c) ________ d) ________

17) $10x = 1000$ a) b) c) ________ d) ________

18) $7y = 98$ a) b) c) ________ d) ________

Name ______________________________ Date ______________________________

Learning About Parentheses and Brackets

Many equations will have parentheses and/or brackets that must be removed before solving the equation. When removing parentheses and brackets, it is very important to remember that when the parentheses are preceded by a positive sign (+) the signs inside the parentheses **are not** changed.

Example:

Begin with the equation: $2 + (5x - 1) = 11$
Remove parentheses and multiply each term inside by 1. $2 + 5x \bullet 1 - 1 \bullet 1 = 11$
The equation becomes: $2 + 5x - 1 = 11$
Subtract -2 and +1 from each side of the equation. $+2 - 2 + 5x - 1 + 1 = 11 - 2 + 1$
The equation becomes: $5x = 10$
Divide each side of the equation by 5. $5x \div 5 = 10 \div 5$
Which means $x = 2$

Example:

Begin with the equation $3 + (2x + 1) = 16$
Becomes $3 + 2x + 1 = 16$
Becomes $-3 + 3 + 2x + 1 - 1 = 16 - 3 - 1$
Becomes $\frac{2x}{2} = \frac{12}{2}$
Becomes $x = 6$
Check $3 + 2 \bullet 6 + 1 = 16$ $(16 = 16)$

Solve the following. The first one has been completed.

1) $5 + 2(x + 2) = 21$
a) $5 + 2x + 4 = 21$
b) $-5 + 5 + 2x + 4 - 4 = 21 - 5 - 4$
c) $\frac{2x}{2} = \frac{12}{2}$
d) $x = 6$
e) check: $5 + 2 \bullet 6 + 4 = 21$ $(21 = 21)$

2) $1 + (3x - 3) = 1$
a)
b)
c)
d) ____________
e) check: ______________________

3) $8 + 3(y + 2) = 20$
a)
b)
c)
d) ____________
e) check: ______________________

4) $-3 + 2(y - 3) = -3$
a)
b)
c)
d) ____________
e) check: ______________________

Name ______________________ Date ______________________

Learning About Parentheses and Brackets (continued)

It is also important to remember that when the parentheses are preceded by a negative sign (-), the signs inside the parentheses **are** changed.

Example:

Begin with the equation: $2 - (5x - 1) = -7$

Remove parentheses and multiply each term inside by -1.

$2 + 5x \bullet (-1) - 1 \bullet (-1) = -7$

The equation becomes: $2 - 5x + 1 = -7$

Subtract -2 and -1 from each side of the equation. $-2 + 2 - 5x + 1 - 1 = -7 - 2 - 1$

The equation becomes: $-5x = -10$

Divide each side of the equation by -5. $\frac{-5x}{-5} = \frac{-10}{-5}$

Which means: $x = 2$

Example:

Begin with the equation: $3 - (2x + 1) = -16$

Becomes: $3 - 2x - 1 = -16$

Becomes: $-3 + 3 - 2x - 1 + 1 = -16 - 3 + 1$

Becomes: $-2x = -18$

Becomes: $\frac{-2x}{-2} = \frac{-18}{-2}$

Becomes: $x = 9$

Check: $3 - (2 \bullet 9 + 1) = -16$

Solve the following. The first one has been completed.

5) $5 - 2(x + 2) = -9$

a) $5 - 2x - 4 = -9$

b) $-5 + 5 - 2x - 4 + 4 = -9 - 5 + 4$

c) $\frac{-2x}{-2} = \frac{-10}{-2}$

d) $x = 5$ __________

e) check: $5 - 2 \bullet 5 - 4 = -9$ __________

6) $3 - 6(x + 3) = 33$

a)

b)

c)

d) __________

e) check: __________

7) $-4(2x - 2) = -16$

a)

b)

c)

d) __________

e) check: __________

8) $3x - (2x + 4) = -2$

a)

b)

c)

d) __________

e) check: __________

Name ________________________ Date ________________________

Order of Operations

When solving equations, the order of operations is very important. The operations are addition, subtraction, multiplication, and division.

When equations have mathematical expressions with parentheses, it is important to remove the parentheses before performing the operations. You have learned that when the parentheses are preceded by a positive sign, the signs inside the parentheses are not changed when the parentheses are removed. When the parentheses are preceded by a negative sign, the signs inside the parentheses are changed when the parentheses are removed.

Example 1:

In an equation or mathematical expression, begin with the equation:

$3 - (7 + 3) + (\frac{2}{2}) = x$

1. Work from left to right $3 - (7 + 3) + (\frac{2}{2}) = x$
2. Left to right remove parentheses/attach correct signs $3 - 7 - 3 + \frac{2}{2} = x$
3. From left to right complete any multiplication and division $3 - 7 - 3 + 1 = x$
4. From left to right complete the addition and subtraction $3 - 7 - 3 + 1 = x$
5. Which means: $-6 = x$
6. Simplify if necessary.

Simplify the following: The first one has been completed.

1) $5 - (6 + 2) + 3(2) = x$
   a) $5 - 6 - 2 + 3(2) = x$
   b) $5 - 6 - 2 + 6 = x$
   c) $3 = x$

2) $8 - (4 + 3 + 1) + (\frac{8}{4}) = x$
   a)
   b)
   c)
   d)

3) $10 + (8 + 1) - 2(-5) = x$
   a)
   b)
   c)
   d)

4) $-1(6) + -2(\frac{8}{4}) = x$
   a)
   b)
   c)
   d)

5) $(3 \bullet 3) - (\frac{10}{5}) + 2 = x$
   a)
   b)
   c)
   d)

6) $-1 + 4 - 7 + 2 - 5 = x$
   a)
   b)
   c)
   d)

Name ______________________________ Date ______________________________

Order of Operations (continued)

7) $1(6) + 2(\frac{8}{4}) = x$
a)
b)
c)
d)

8) $8 + (4 - 3 - 1) - (\frac{8}{4}) = x$
a)
b)
c)
d)

9) $-6 + 5(-7 \cdot 7) - (\frac{10}{5}) = x$
a)
b)
c)
d)

10) $3(\frac{40}{10}) - 2(\frac{6}{3}) = x$
a)
b)
c)
d)

Example 2 :

Begin with the equation: $6a(3 + 1) + \frac{28}{7} = x$

1) Left to right remove parentheses/attach correct signs: $18a + 6a + \frac{28}{7} = x$
2) Left to right complete any multiplication/division: $18a + 6a + 4 = x$
3) Left to right complete addition/subtraction $24a + 4 = x$
4) Simplify if necessary $4(6a + 1) = x$

Simplify the following.

11) $5(x - y) - z = x$
a)
b)
c)
d)

12) $9x - 2(3a + a) - 3(\frac{4}{2}a) = x$
a)
b)
c)
d)

13) $(\frac{25}{5}x) -2(3 + 4x) = x$
a)
b)
c)
d)

14) $12 - x(6 - 1) + 20 \div (-2) = x$
a)
b)
c)
d)

15) $3z - 4(a + b) + x/y = x$
a)
b)
c)
d)

16) $-4x - (8 \cdot 3) = x$
a)
b)
c)
d)

Name ______________________ Date ______________________

Quiz VI: Learning About Equations

Fill in the blanks in the following selection with the appropriate word chosen from the list below.

equality	**algebraic expressions**	**$2x + 1 = 7$**	**parentheses**
left/right	**operations**	**addition**	**subtraction**
multiplication	**division**	**added**	**subtracted**
divided	**multiplied**	**simplified**	**equal**
zero	**positive**	**negative**	
mathematical statement			

An equation is a (1) ____________ ______________ of (2) _______, like (3)___+__ =___ . An equation is made up of two (4) ___________ ___________ connected by the (5)_____ sign, which is the sign of (6) ________.

The same number may be (7) _________ to each side of an equation without changing the equation. The same number may be (8) _________ from each side of an equation without changing the equation. Excepting for 9)____ , each side of the equation may be multiplied or (10)________ by the same number without changing the equation.

In simplifying an equation, one must always work from (11) _____ to _____ . First the (12) ____________ are removed. When the parentheses are preceded by a (13) __________ sign, the signs inside the parentheses are changed when the parentheses are removed. When the parentheses are preceded by a 14)_________ sign, the signs inside the parentheses are not changed when the parentheses are removed.

Once the parentheses have been removed, the order of operations from (15)____ to _____ are first (16) ___________ and _________ and then 17) ___________ and _______________ . Following the operations, the terms are combined and the resulting mathematical expression is (18) __________.

Simplify the following :

19) $6x - (2 - x) + 3 = x$ ______________________________

20) $2y + (\frac{10}{5}x) - 2(3 + 1) = x$ ______________________________

Match the the definition in Column B with the corresponding item in Column A.

	Column A	**Column B**
_____	21) $6y + 1 = 13$	A. Monomial
_____	22) $6x$	B. Algebraic expression
_____	23) $6a + 1$	C. Equation
_____	24) $6y + 2$	D. Cannot be used to divide each side of an equation
_____	25) Zero	E. Simplified is $2(3y + 1)$

Name ______________________________ Date ______________________________

Understanding and Using Exponents

There are times when a number is used as a factor several times. A number may be multiplied by itself once or several times. To multiply a number by itself once is called **squaring** a number. This also may be called raising the number to its **second power.** If the number is multiplied by itself three times, we say the number is raised to its **third power** and so on. The power of a number is the product resulting from multiplying a number by itself a number of times. Raising a number to a specific power is exactly the *opposite* process of finding the root of a number.

5 • 5 =	25	Five to the second power, also called five squared
5 • 5 • 5 =	125	Five to the third power, also called five cubed
5 • 5 • 5 • 5 =	625	Five to the fourth power
5 • 5 • 5 • 5 • 5 =	3,125	Five to the sixth power

In order to make this process easy to write and easy to understand, mathematicians have devised a kind of a shorthand method of indicating that a number should be used as a factor more than once. They write the number along with an exponent. The number or variable with the exponent is called the **base.** The **exponent** number is smaller and is placed above and behind the first. The exponent shows how many times the first number should be used as a factor. Sometimes you will find a variable like *x* or *y* with an exponent, as with x^3 or y^7. In this example, the bases are the numbers assigned to *x* and *y*. The exponents are 3 and 7.

Base ——> 5^4 <—— Exponent

Using the above examples, here is how the numbers should be written with exponents.

5 • 5	= 5^2 =	Five to the second power
5 • 5 • 5	= 5^3 =	Five to the third power
5 • 5 • 5 • 5	= 5^4 =	Five to the fourth power
5 • 5 • 5 • 5 • 5	= 5^5 =	Five to the fifth power

The exponent for each of the numbers below indicates how many times the number should be used as a factor. For each of the following, fill in the blank with the standard number. The first one has been completed.

1) 4^3 = 64 2) 3^3 = ______

3) 7^2 = ______ 4) 10^5 = ______

5) 14^3 = ______ 6) 8^8 = ______

7) 11^7 = ______ 8) 7^9 = ______

9) 6^6 = ______ 10) 12^5 = ______

Name ______________________________ Date ______________________________

Exponents, Bases, and Factors

When learning about exponents, it is important to know the meaning of the terms **exponent, base,** and **factor.**

- **Exponent:** The small number appearing to the right and above a number or variable.

  For example, 4^2, 3^5, 7^3, 10^4, x^9, y^6, $2x^3$, 4^5x^2 are all either a number, a variable, or a number and variable with exponents. The exponent is the small number to the right and above the number or variable.

- **Base:** The number or variable with the exponent is called the base.

  For example the numbers, variables, or numbers and variables in bold are each a base: $\mathbf{4}^2$, $\mathbf{3}^5$, $\mathbf{7}^3$, $\mathbf{10}^4$, $\boldsymbol{x}^9$, $\boldsymbol{y}^6$, $\mathbf{2}\boldsymbol{x}^3$, $\mathbf{4}^5\boldsymbol{x}^2$.

- **Factor:** The numbers that are multiplied together to get a product.

  For example, 3 and 2 are factors of 6 because $3 \bullet 2 = 6$. The factors 3 and 4 are factors of 12 because $3 \bullet 4 = 12$. Three is a factor of 9 because $3 \bullet 3 = 9$.

The **exponent** tells you how many times the **base** is to be multiplied as a **factor**. For example, 2^2 tells you to multiply $2 \bullet 2 = 4$, 2^3 tells you to multiply $2 \bullet 2 \bullet 2 = 8$, 4^4 tells you to multiply $4 \bullet 4 \bullet 4 \bullet 4 = 256$

Sometimes you will find a variable like *x* or *y* with an exponent, for example, x^2 or y^2. In this case the base is the number assigned for *x* or *y*.

Solve the following:

1) $2^2 =$ ______	2) $2^3 =$ ______	3) $2^4 =$ ______	4) $2^6 =$ ______
5) $3^2 =$ ______	6) $3^3 =$ ______	7) $3^4 =$ ______	8) $3^5 =$ ______
9) $4^2 =$ ______	10) $4^3 =$ ______	11) $4^4 =$ ______	12) $4^5 =$ ______
13) $10^2 =$ ______	14) $10^3 =$ ______	15) $10^4 =$ ______	16) $10^5 =$ ______

Name ______________________________ Date ______________________________

Exponents in Algebraic Expressions

Algebraic expressions are often written with variables and exponents.

Example: x^2, y^4, $x^2 + 1$

When a variable appears with an exponent, the variable must be assigned a numerical value before the problem can be solved.

Example: To solve x^2, a numerical value must be assigned to the variable x.
Let x equal 5. Then $x^2 = 5^2 = 25$. If x equals 3, then $x^2 = 3^2 = 9$

Solve the following:

1) $x = 2$ then $x^2 =$ ______ 2) $x = 3$ then $x^3 =$ ______ 3) $x = 5$ then $x^5 =$ ______

4) $y = 3$ then $y^3 + 1 =$ ____ 5) $y = 4$ then $y^4 - 1 =$ ____ 6) $x = 2$; $y = 2$ then $x^2 + y^2 =$ ____

7) $x = 3$ then $x^2 + x =$ ____ 8) $y = 4$ then $y^3 - y =$ ____ 9) $t = 4$ then $t^2 =$ ______

The following algebraic expressions include constants, variables, and exponents.

To solve the following, let $x = 4$; $y = 3$

10) $3x^2 =$ ____________ 11) $4y^3 =$ __________

12) $2x^3 + 2 =$ __________ 13) $3x^2 + 2y =$ ____________

Solve the following: $x = 5$; $y = 3$

14) $\frac{2x^2}{2} + 3y^2 =$ ________ 15) $4x^3 - \frac{y^3}{9} + 2 =$ ___________ 16) $\frac{1}{x^2} + y^2 =$ ___________

Name ______________________________ Date ______________________________

Looking for Patterns When Using Exponents

Write the answer to each of the following on the blank next to the problem. The first one has been completed.

1) 3^1 = 3   2) 3^2 = ____   3) 3^3 = ____   4) 3^4 = ____

Answer the following questions

5) The answer in Problem 2 is a) 1 b) 2 c)3 d) 4 times greater than the answer in Problem 1.
6) The answer in Problem 3 is a) 1 b) 2 c)3 d) 4 times greater than the answer in Problem 2.
7)The answer in Problem 4 is a) 1 b) 2 c)3 d) 4 times greater than the answer in Problem 3.
8) The answer to the problem 3^5 will be _____ times the answer to 3^4.

In each of the following problems fill in the blanks with the numbers indicated by letter to form a fraction. Each number corresponds to a letter: a, b, c, d, or e. The first one has been completed.

a) $3^5 = 243$ b) $3^4 = 81$ c)$3^3 = 27$ d)$3^2 = 9$ e)$3^1 = 3$

9) $\frac{b}{a} = \frac{81}{243}$ 10) $\frac{c}{b}$ = ____   11) $\frac{d}{c}$ = ____   12) $\frac{e}{d}$ = ____

Change each of the fractions in Problems 9–12 to a simple fraction.

13) $\frac{81}{243}$ = ____   14) $\frac{27}{81}$ = ____   15) $\frac{9}{27}$ = ____   16) $\frac{3}{9}$ = ____

Complete the following: Remember the fraction for f/e must equal $\frac{1}{3}$.

17a) $3^5 = 243$ b) $3^4 = 81$ c)$3^3 = 27$ d)$3^2 = 9$ e)$3^1 = 3$ f) 3^0 = ____

When working with exponents it is important to remember that any base with an exponent of 0 is equal to 1. $3^0 = 1$ $x^0 = 1$

Complete the following

18a) 2^0 = ___ b) 3^0 = ___ c) 4^0 = ___ d) 5^0 = ___ e) 6^0 = ___ f) 7^0 = ___ g) 8^0 = ___

Solve the following:

19a) 2^5 = ___ b) 2^4 = ___ c) 2^3 = ___ d) 2^2 = ___ e) 2^1 = ___ f) 2^0 = ___

20) When the exponent for the base numeral 2 is *decreased* by 1 the answer is
a) $\frac{1}{3}$ b) $\frac{1}{2}$ c) $\frac{1}{4}$ d) $\frac{1}{5}$ the original exponent.

Name ______________________ Date ______________________

Expressing Exponents in Words

In the study of mathematics, the base and exponent are read in a particular way.

Example: 2^2 is read as "two to the second power." Note the base is read as the numeral it represents. The exponent is read as "to a power."

Example: 5^3 is read as "five to the third power."

In the blanks beside each base and exponent, write the statement that the term describes. The first one has been completed.

1) 3^2 is read as: Three to the second power.

2) 5^3 is read as: ______________________

3) 4^4 is read as: ______________________

4) 10^3 is read as: ______________________

5) 7^5 is read as: ______________________

6) 42^1 is read as: ______________________

In blank a) place the base and exponent the statement describes. In blank b) place the number the base and exponent represent. The first one is completed.

7) Eight to the second power. a) 8^2 equals b) 64

8) Twelve to the eighth power. a) ________ equals b) ________

9) Two to the sixth power. a) ________ equals b) ________

10) Four to the zero power. a) ________ equals b) ________

11) Six to the second power. a) ________ equals b) ________

12) Three to the fourth power. a) ________ equals b) ________

13) Seven to the first power. a) ________ equals b) ________

14) Five to the third power. a) ________ equals b) ________

15) Twenty-five to the fifth power. a) ________ equals b) ________

Name ______________________________ Date ____________________________

Dealing With Negative Exponents and Negative Bases

All of the base numbers previously have had positive exponents. However, many base numbers will have negative exponents. In the example below all of the base two numerals in bold have a negative exponent.

2^5 2^4 2^3 2^2 2^1 2^0 $\mathbf{2^{-1}}$ $\mathbf{2^{-2}}$ $\mathbf{2^{-3}}$ $\mathbf{2^{-4}}$ $\mathbf{2^{-5}}$

You have learned how to handle base numbers with a positive exponent. The rule for using negative exponents is: **Rewrite the base and exponent as a fraction with a numerator of one. Note that the exponent and base will both be positive.**

Example: 2^{-2} is rewritten as $\frac{1}{2^2}$ or $\frac{1}{4}$; 4^{-3} is rewritten as $\frac{1}{4^3}$ or $\frac{1}{64}$

Rewrite the following. In blank a) write the base and negative exponent as a fraction with a numerator of one. In blank b) rewrite the fraction without the exponent. The first one has been completed.

1) $2^{-2} = \frac{1}{2^2} = \frac{1}{4}$ 2) 3^{-4} = ____ = ____ 3) 4^{-3} = ____ = ____

4) 6^{-3} = ____ = ____ 5) 5^{-3} = ____ = ____ 6) 10^{-2} = ____ = ____

Sometimes exponents will be found with a negative base numeral. It will be important to use the following rules.

When a *positive base* number is raised to an even or odd power, the base number will always remain positive.

Example: $2^2 = 4$; $2^3 = 8$; $2^4 = 16$; $2^5 = 32$; $2^6 = 64$

When a *negative base* number is raised to an even power, the base number will become positive.

Example: $-2^2 = 4$; $-2^4 = 16$; $-2^6 = 64$; $-2^8 = 256$; $-2^{10} = 1{,}024$

When a *negative base* number is raised to an odd power, the base number will remain negative.

Example: $-2^3 = -8$; $-2^5 = -32$; $-2^7 = -128$; $-2^9 = -512$

Solve the following.

7) -3^2 = ______ 8) -3^5 = ______ 9) 3^3 = ______ 10) -4^3 = ______ 11) 5^3 = ______

12) -2^9 = ______ 13) -8^3 = ______ 14) -5^2 = ______ 15) -2^4 = ______

Name ______________________ Date ______________________

Adding, Subtracting, and Multiplying Exponents

Variables and numbers with exponents will occur frequently in algebraic expressions.

When the *base numbers* or *variables* are the same, the exponents can be added.

In problems where you are multiplying numbers or variables with the same base, the exponents can be added. To multiply powers of the same base, add their exponents.

Examples: 3^2 times $3^1 = 3^2 \bullet 3^1 = 3^{2+1} = 3^3$; $3 \bullet 3 \bullet 3 = 27$

x^2 times $x^2 = x^2 \bullet x^2 = x^{2+2} = x^4$

$5^3 \bullet 5^2 = 5^5$
$5^3 = 125$; $5^2 = 25$
$5^3 \bullet 5^2 = 5^{3+2} = 5^5 = 3{,}125$
$25 \bullet 125 = 3{,}125$

Note in all of the examples the **bases** or **variables** to be multiplied were the same.

Solve the following multiplication problems. Add the exponents and raise the base number to the indicated exponent. Place the answers on the blanks a), b), and c). Only a) and b) can be answered for those with variables. The first one is completed.

1) $5^2 \bullet 5^1 =$ exponents added equals a) 5^{2+1} rewritten as b) 5^3 equals c) 125
2) $6^3 \bullet 6^2 =$ exponents added equals a) _____ rewritten as b) ____ equals c) ________
3) $7^3 \bullet 7^5 =$ exponents added equals a) _____ rewritten as b) ____ equals c) ________
4) $x^3 \bullet x^2 =$ exponents added equals a) _____ rewritten as b) ____
5) $y^1 \bullet y^4 =$ exponents added equals a) _____ rewritten as b) ____
6) $r^4 \bullet r^2 =$ exponents added equals a) _____ rewritten as b) ____

Many times exponents will appear in algebraic expressions like the following.

$(4^2)^2$ or $(a^2)^3$

One can solve $(4^2)^2$ by first raising the 4 inside the parentheses to the second power and then raising the answer to the second power.

$(4 \bullet 4)^2 = (16)^2 = 16 \bullet 16 = 256$

However, there is another way to solve this problem. You can multiply the exponents and then solve the problem.

$(4^2)^2 = 4^{2 \bullet 2} = 4^4 = 4 \bullet 4 \bullet 4 \bullet 4 = 256$

Name ______________________________ Date ______________________

Adding, Subtracting, and Multiplying Exponents (continued)

Raise the base number or variable to the indicated power by multiplying the exponents. The first one has been completed.

7) $(2^2)^3$ = a) $2^{2 \cdot 3}$ = b) 2^6 = c) 64

8) $(2^4)^2$ = a) ______ = b) ______ = c) ______

9) $(10^3)^2$ = a) ______ = b) ______ = c) ______

10) $(7^1)^5$ = a) ______ = b) ______ = c) ______

11) $(5^3)^3$ = a) ______ = b) ______ = c) ______

12) $(12^2)^2$ = a) ______ = b) ______ = c) ______

13) $(3^3)^4$ = a) ______ = b) ______ = c) ______

14) If "a" equals 2 then $(a^5)^2$ = a) ______ = b) ______ = c) ______

15) If "x" equals 3 then $(x^2)^2$ = a) ______ = b) ______ = c) ______

16) If "y" equals 6 then $(y^1)^3$ = a) ______ = b) ______ = c) ______

Numbers or variables with exponents are often found in division problems, as well.

When dividing numbers or variables with exponents, the exponent in the dividend is subtracted from the exponent in the divisor.

Example: $5^3 \div 5^2 = 5^{3-2} = 5^1 = 5$ or $5^2 \div 5^3 = 5^{2-3} = 5^{-1} = \frac{1}{5^1} = \frac{1}{5}$

$x^5 \div x^2 = x^{5-2} = x^3$ or $x^3 \div x^5 = x^{3-5} = x^{-2} = \frac{1}{x^2}$

Solve the following. The first one has been completed.

17) $6^4 \div 6^2$ = a) 6^{4-2} = b) 6^2 = c) 36

18) $7^5 \div 7^4$ = a) ______ = b) ______ = c) ______

19) $2^6 \div 2^3$ = a) ______ = b) ______ = c) ______

20) $4^2 \div 4^5$ = a) ______ = b) ______ = c) ______ = d) ______

21) $3^1 \div 3^6$ = a) ______ = b) ______ = c) ______ = d) ______

22) $x^4 \div x^2$ = a) ______ = b) ______

23) $y^6 \div y^3$ = a) ______ = b) ______

24) $x^4 \div x^6$ = a) ______ = b) ______ = c) ______

25) $y^7 \div y^8$ = a) ______ = b) ______ = c) ______

Name ______________________________ Date ___________________________

Quiz VII: Understanding and Using Exponents

Write the statement that describes how the base and exponent would be read aloud.

1) 4^6 = ____

2) 3^5 = ____

3) 2^4 = ____

Write the number of factors in each expression on blank a) and list the factors on blank b).

4) 5^3 a) _____ b) _______________ 5) 10^5 a) _____ b) _______________

6) 3^6 a) _____ b) _______________ 7) y^4 a) _____ b) _______________

Raise each of the following to the indicated power

8) 5^3 = _____ 9) 4^0 = _____ 10) 10^4 = _____ 11) 2^6 = _____ 12) 4^3 = _____

Raise each of the variables to the indicated power.

13) If $x = 4$, then x^2 = ____ 14) If $y = 9$, then y^0 = ____ 15) If t equals 5, then t^3 = ______

Solve the following.

16) If $x = 2$, then $3x^2$ = ___ 17) If $y = 3$, then $10y^3$ = ___ 18) If t equals 4, then $6t^2$ = ___

Rewrite each of the following as a fraction with a numerator of one. Raise the base to the indicated power.

19) 2^{-2} = ____ = ____ 20) 3^{-1} = ____ = ____ 21) 5^{-2} = ____ = ____

Complete the following.

22) 5^4 = ___ 5^3 = ___ 5^2 = ___ 5^1 = ___ 5^0 = ___ 5^{-1} = ___ 5^{-2} = ___ 5^{-3} = ___ 5^{-4} = ___

Refer to Question 22 and answer the following.

23) Increasing the exponent by one increases the numerical value of the base number five

a) 2 times b) 5 times c) 3 times d) 4 times

24) Write the simple fraction represented by a) $5^3/5^4$ ______ b) $5^2/5^3$ ______

Solve the following.

25) $9^2 \bullet 9^5$ = ______________________ 26) $11^4 \bullet 11^1$ = ______________________

27) $(5^4)^2$ = ______________________ 28) $(7^2)^3$ = ______________________

29) $4^8 \div 4^2$ = ______________________ 30) $4^2 \div 4^8$ = ______________________

Name ______________________________ Date ____________________________

Learning about Radicals and Roots

Radicals are often used in algebra in order to solve problems. Before you can solve such problems, it is necessary to find the root of the numbers or variables under the radical.

The $\sqrt{}$ is the **radical sign**. The number or variable under the radical sign is the **radicand.** The **index** is the number that indicates the root that is to be found. The index indicates that you are to find the square root, cube root, fourth root, fifth root, and so on.

Index

$\sqrt[3]{125}$ —— Radicand

Radical

In the study of exponents, a number is *raised* to a given power.

Example: 5 raised to the second power is written as 5^2 or 5 • 5 which equals 25.
So 5 raised to the second power is $5^2 = 25$

The inverse operation of raising a number to a power is extracting the root of a number.

Example: Find the square root of 25. **The square root is the number that multiplied times itself will produce 25.**

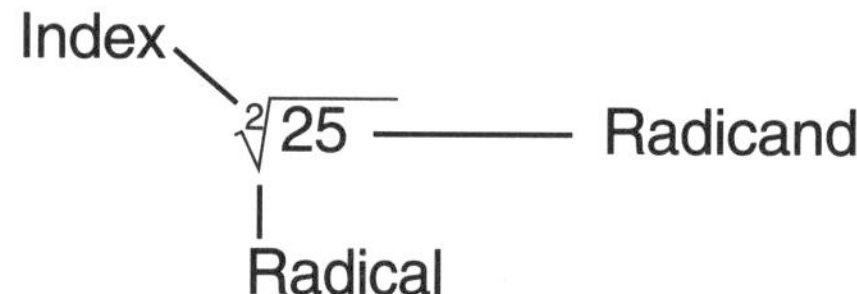

In the above example the radical is the sign $\sqrt{}$.
The radicand is the number 25.
The index is the number 2 indicating the square root.
Solution: The square root of 25 is 5. 5 • 5 = 25

The index is a very important number used in the process of finding the root. The index tells the root that is to be found. The index for the square root is the number 2. Often this index is omitted. Therefore, when the square root is to be found, the index 2 will usually not appear in the radical. In all other roots, such as the cube root or the fourth root, the index number must be included in the radical.

Name ______________________________ Date ______________________________

Learning How to Read and Write Radicals

Examples:

$\sqrt[2]{4}$ or $\sqrt{4}$ says "find the square root of 4." = 2 ($2^2 = 2 \cdot 2 = 4$)

$\sqrt[3]{8}$ says, "find the cube root of 8." = 2 ($2^3 = 2 \cdot 2 \cdot 2 = 8$)

$\sqrt[4]{16}$ says, "find the fourth root of 16." = 2 ($2^4 = 2 \cdot 2 \cdot 2 \cdot 2 = 16$)

$\sqrt[5]{32}$ says, "find the fifth root of 32." = 2 ($2^5 = 2 \cdot 2 \cdot 2 \cdot 2 \cdot 2 = 32$)

$\sqrt[6]{64}$ says, "find the sixth root of 64." = 2 ($2^6 = 2 \cdot 2 \cdot 2 \cdot 2 \cdot 2 \cdot 2 = 64$)

Complete the following. The first one is completed.

1) $\sqrt{25}$ says, "find the square root of 25."
2) $\sqrt[4]{64}$ says, ______________________________
3) $\sqrt[3]{8}$ says, ______________________________
4) $\sqrt{16}$ says, ______________________________
5) $\sqrt[5]{625}$ says, ______________________________
6) $\sqrt{100}$ says, ______________________________
7) $\sqrt[3]{81}$ says, ______________________________
8) $\sqrt[8]{256}$ says, ______________________________
9) $\sqrt[6]{729}$ says, ______________________________
10) $\sqrt{5}$ says, ______________________________

Complete the following. For each of the statements draw a radical on the blank, place the correct index in the radical, and place the radicand under the radical. The first one has been completed.

11) Indicates that the square root of 64 is to be found. $\sqrt[2]{64}$ or $\sqrt{64}$
12) Indicates that the cube root of 125 is to be found. ______________
13) Indicates that the fourth root of 64 is to be found. ______________
14) Indicates that the eighth root of 256 is to be found ______________
15) Indicates that the fifth root of 1,024 is to be found. ______________
16) Indicates that the square root of 3 is to be found. ______________
17) Indicates that the square root of 2 is to be found. ______________
18) Indicates that the cube root of 27 is to be found. ______________
19) Indicates that the fourth root of 81 is to be found. ______________
20) Indicates that the cube root of 1,000 is to be found. ______________

Name ______________________ Date ______________________

Number of Factors

When finding the root of a number, you are finding how many times the number should be used as a factor when that number is the only factor used.

Example: Find the square root of 25. $\sqrt{25} = 5 \bullet 5$ (five used as a factor two times)
Find the cube root of 125. $\sqrt[3]{125} = 5 \bullet 5 \bullet 5$ (five used as a factor three times)
Find the sixth root of 64. $\sqrt[6]{64} = 2 \bullet 2 \bullet 2 \bullet 2 \bullet 2 \bullet 2$ (two used as a factor six times)

Complete the following. Find the indicated root and write the answer on the blank a), and on blank b) indicate the number of times the answer is to be used as a factor. The first one has been completed for you.

1) $\sqrt[4]{81}$ = a) 3 b) $3 \bullet 3 \bullet 3 \bullet 3$
2) $\sqrt[3]{125}$ = a)______ b) ______________________
3) $\sqrt[4]{256}$ = a)______ b) ______________________
4) $\sqrt[5]{1{,}024}$ = a)______ b ______________________
5) $\sqrt[2]{9}$ = a)______ b) ______________________

All of the problems you have solved so far resulted in a **rational** number. However, there are times when the root of a problem is found that the answer is an **irrational** number.

***Rational* numbers are numbers that can be written as the quotient of fractions. Rational numbers can be expressed with finite, non-repeating decimals or with repeating decimals. Examples: a) $\frac{3}{4} = 0.75$ b) $\frac{2}{3} = 0.666666666666...$**

***Irrational* numbers are numbers that cannot be written as fractions. Irrational numbers are infinite, non-repeating decimals. When an irrational number is written in decimal form, the decimal is an endless, non-repeating decimal. An irrational number is a number with an infinite number of digits. 3.14159265... is a non-repeating decimal. It is an irrational number.**

Solve the following. Write the answer on blank a), the term rational or irrational on blank b), and the number of times the answer is used as a factor on blank c). The first one has been completed.

6) $\sqrt[2]{2}$ = a) 1.414213562... b) irrational c) 2
7) $\sqrt[2]{3}$ = a) ______________ b) ______________ c) ______
8) $\sqrt[5]{25}$ = a) ______________ b) ______________ c) ______
9) $\sqrt[3]{8}$ = a) ______________ b) ______________ c) ______
10) $\sqrt[2]{38}$ = a) ______________ b) ______________ c) ______

Name ______________________ Date ______________________

Adding Radicals

Many algebraic expressions include radicals. Often an algebraic expression will include more than one radical. It is often easier to solve problems with more than one radical if the radicals in the expression can be combined.

Radicals can be added if the indexes and radicands are the same.

Example 1: $2\sqrt{5} + 4\sqrt{5}$ can be added. The radicands are both the same (5), and both indexes indicate the square root is to be found.

Example 2: $2\sqrt{5} + 4\sqrt[3]{5}$ cannot be added. The radicands are the same, but the first radicand has an index for the square root, and the second radicand has an index for the cube root.

When adding radicals, the **coefficients** are added. In Example 1 above the coefficients are the numbers **2** and **4.**

Step 1: Add the coefficients: 2 + 4

Step 2: Rewrite the answer as: $6\sqrt{5}$

$$2\sqrt{5} + 4\sqrt{5} = 2 + 4 = 6\sqrt{5}$$

When the radical has a coefficient of 1, the number 1 is not written before the radical. However, when adding it is added as 1.

Example: $3\sqrt{4} + \sqrt{4} = 3 + 1\sqrt{4} = 4\sqrt{4}$

Solve the following problems: The first one has been completed.

1) $4\sqrt{9} + 3\sqrt{9} =$ __4__ + __$3\sqrt{9}$__ = __$7\sqrt{9}$__
2) $2\sqrt{5} + \sqrt{5} =$ ____ + ____$\sqrt{}$ = ___$\sqrt{}$
3) $5\sqrt{13} + \sqrt{13} =$ ____ + ____$\sqrt{}$ = ___$\sqrt{}$
4) $12\sqrt{156} + 3\sqrt{156} =$ ___ + ____$\sqrt{}$ = ___$\sqrt{}$
5) $3\sqrt{7} + 3\sqrt{7} =$ ____ + ____$\sqrt{}$ = ___$\sqrt{}$
6) $5\sqrt{8} + 3\sqrt{8} =$ ____ + ____$\sqrt{}$ = ___$\sqrt{}$
7) $\sqrt{5} + 7\sqrt{5} =$ ____ + ____$\sqrt{}$ = ___$\sqrt{}$
8) $\sqrt{2} + \sqrt{2} =$ ____ + ____$\sqrt{}$ = ___$\sqrt{}$
9) $\sqrt{2} + \sqrt{2} + 3\sqrt{2} =$ ____ + ____ + ____$\sqrt{}$ = ___$\sqrt{}$
10) $\sqrt{5} + \sqrt{5} + 3\sqrt{5} =$ ____ + ____ + ____$\sqrt{}$ = ___$\sqrt{}$
11) $\sqrt{7} + \sqrt{7} + 8\sqrt{7} =$ ____ + ____ + ____$\sqrt{}$ = ___$\sqrt{}$
12) $\sqrt{2} + \sqrt{2} + 4\sqrt{2} =$ ____ + ____ + ____$\sqrt{}$ = ___$\sqrt{}$

Name ______________________________ Date ______________________

SUBTRACTING RADICALS

Radicals can be subtracted if the indexes and radicands are the same. When subtracting radicals, the coefficients are subtracted.

Example: $5\sqrt{7} - 3\sqrt{7}$ can be subtracted. The indexes are the same and the radicands are the same.

Step 1: Subtract the coefficients: 5 - 3 = 2

Step 2: Rewrite as $2\sqrt{7}$

$$5\sqrt{7} - 3\sqrt{7} = 5 - 3 = 2\sqrt{7}$$

When the radical has a coefficient of 1, the number 1 is not written before the radical. However, when subtracting it is subtracted as 1.

Example: $3\sqrt{4} - \sqrt{4} = 3 - 1\sqrt{4} = 2\sqrt{4}$

Solve the following. The first one has been completed.

1) $7\sqrt{5} - 4\sqrt{5}$ = <u>7</u> - <u>4</u>$\sqrt{}$ = <u>3</u>$\sqrt{2}$
2) $5\sqrt{7} - 4\sqrt{7}$ = ____ - ____$\sqrt{}$ = ____$\sqrt{}$
3) $9\sqrt{3} - 4\sqrt{3}$ = ____ - ____$\sqrt{}$ = ____$\sqrt{}$
4) $9\sqrt{8} - \sqrt{8}$ = ____ - ____$\sqrt{}$ = ____$\sqrt{}$
5) $\sqrt{12} - \sqrt{12}$ = ____ - ____$\sqrt{}$ = ____$\sqrt{}$
6) $6\sqrt{4} - 5\sqrt{4}$ = ____ - ____$\sqrt{}$ = ____$\sqrt{}$
7) $6\sqrt{10} - 3\sqrt{10} - 2\sqrt{10}$ = ____ - ____ - ____$\sqrt{}$ = ____$\sqrt{}$
8) $10\sqrt{2} - 6\sqrt{2} - \sqrt{2}$ = ____ - ____ - ____$\sqrt{}$ = ____$\sqrt{}$
9) $4\sqrt{16} - 7\sqrt{16}$ = ____ - ____$\sqrt{}$ = ____$\sqrt{}$
10) $8\sqrt{9} - 5\sqrt{9}$ = ____ - ____$\sqrt{}$ = ____$\sqrt{}$

Solve the following problems. These problems include addition and subtraction steps.

11) $6\sqrt{10} + 3\sqrt{10} - 2\sqrt{10}$ = ____ + ____ - ____$\sqrt{}$ = ____$\sqrt{}$
12) $\sqrt{3} + 3\sqrt{3} - 2\sqrt{3}$ = ____ + ____ - ____$\sqrt{}$ = ____$\sqrt{}$
13) $5\sqrt{3} - 3\sqrt{3} + 2\sqrt{3}$ = ____ - ____ + ____$\sqrt{}$ = ____$\sqrt{}$
14) $7\sqrt{6} - 4\sqrt{6} + \sqrt{6}$ = ____ - ____ + ____$\sqrt{}$ = ____$\sqrt{}$
15) $\sqrt{20} + 2\sqrt{20} - \sqrt{20}$ = ____ + ____ - ____$\sqrt{}$ = ____$\sqrt{}$

Name ______________________ Date ______________________

Multiplying Radicals

Radicals can be multiplied as you would multiply whole numbers. When multiplying radicals, the *indexes* must be the same. *However*, the radicands can be different numbers or variables.

Example 1: $\sqrt{5} \bullet \sqrt{5} = 5 \bullet 5 = 25$ so $\sqrt{5} \bullet \sqrt{5} = \sqrt{25} = 5$

Example 2: $\sqrt[3]{9} \bullet \sqrt[3]{3} = 9 \bullet 3 = 27$ so $\sqrt[3]{9} \bullet \sqrt[3]{3} = \sqrt[3]{27} = 3$

It is important to note that the indexes are the same in each example.

Solve the following. Complete blank a), b), and c). In blank c) indicate if the answer in blank b) is rational or irrational. If a variable is under the radical, answer only blank a). The first one has been completed.

1) $\sqrt{4} \bullet \sqrt{4} =$ a) $\sqrt{16}$ = b) 4 = c) rational
2) $\sqrt{3} \bullet \sqrt{4} =$ a) $\sqrt{\quad}$ = b) ________ = c) ________
3) $\sqrt{2} \bullet \sqrt{8} =$ a) $\sqrt{\quad}$ = b) ________ = c) ________
4) $3\sqrt{5} \bullet 3\sqrt{25} =$ a) ___$\sqrt{\quad}$ = b) ________ = c) ________
5) $2\sqrt{2} \bullet 2\sqrt{32} =$ a) ___$\sqrt{\quad}$ = b) ________ = c) ________
6) $5\sqrt{x} \bullet 5\sqrt{y} =$ a) ___$\sqrt{\quad}$
7) $2\sqrt{x} \bullet 2\sqrt{y} \bullet 2\sqrt{z} =$ a) ___$\sqrt{\quad}$
8) $4\sqrt{4} \bullet 4\sqrt{6} \bullet 4\sqrt{2} =$ a) ___$\sqrt{\quad}$ = b) ________ = c) ________
9) $\sqrt[4]{3} \bullet 5\sqrt[4]{27} =$ a) ___$\sqrt{\quad}$ = b) ________ = c) ________
10) $\sqrt[3]{2} \bullet \sqrt[3]{4} \bullet 8\sqrt[3]{2} =$ a) ___$\sqrt{\quad}$ = b) ________ = c) ________

Name ______________________________ Date ______________________________

Dividing Radicals

Radicals can be divided as you would divide whole numbers. When dividing radicals, the *indexes* must be the same. However, the radicands can be different numbers or variables.

Example 1: $\sqrt{32} \div \sqrt{2} = \frac{32}{2} = \sqrt{16} = 4$ = rational number
Example 2: $\sqrt{4} \div \sqrt{2} = \frac{4}{2} = \sqrt{2} = 1.414213562$ = irrational number
Example 3: $\sqrt[3]{81} \div \sqrt[3]{3} = \frac{81}{3} = \sqrt[3]{27} = 3$ = rational number

It is important to note that the indexes are the same in each example.

Solve the following. Complete blank a), b), c), and d). Indicate in blank d) whether the answer in blank c) is rational or irrational. If variables are present, you can only complete blanks a) and b). The first one has been completed.

1) $\sqrt{18} \div \sqrt{2} =$ a) $\frac{18}{2}$ = b) $\sqrt{9}$ = c) 3 = d) rational
2) $\sqrt{8} \div \sqrt{2} =$ a) —— = b) $\sqrt{}$ = c) ________ = d) ________
3) $\sqrt{48} \div \sqrt{2} =$ a) —— = b) $\sqrt{}$ = c) ________ = d) ________
4) $\sqrt{16} \div \sqrt{4} =$ a) —— = b) $\sqrt{}$ = c) ________ = d) ________
5) $\sqrt{125} \div \sqrt{5} =$ a) —— = b) $\sqrt{}$ = c) ________ = d) ________
6) $\sqrt[3]{125} \div \sqrt[3]{5} =$ a) —— = b) $\sqrt{}$ = c) ________ = d) ________
7) $\sqrt[5]{64} \div \sqrt[5]{2} =$ a) —— = b) $\sqrt{}$ = c) ________ = d) ________
8) $\sqrt[4]{x} \div \sqrt[4]{y} =$ a) —— = b) $\sqrt{}$
9) $\sqrt{x} \div \sqrt{y} =$ a) —— = b) $\sqrt{}$
10) $\sqrt[3]{x} \div \sqrt[3]{y} =$ a) —— = b) $\sqrt{}$

Name ________________________ Date ________________________

Prime Factors and Simplifying Square Root Radicals

Problems involving **square root radicals** can be written in a **simplified** form in order to solve problems more efficiently. When simplifying square root radicals, it is important to determine the **prime factors of the radicand**.

Prime factors: A **natural number** greater than 1 is **prime** if no number other than 1 and the number itself can divide the number and result in another whole number. When a number is **prime,** it has exactly two factors: the natural number 1 and the number itself.

When finding the prime factors of a number, begin by dividing the number by 2 or 3. Continue dividing by 2 or another natural number until the number left is divisible only by 1 or the number.

Natural numbers: 1, 2, 3, 4, 5, 6, 7, 8, 9, ...

Example 1: Find prime factors for 24. $24 \div \mathbf{2} = 12$ $12 \div \mathbf{2} = 6$ $6 \div \mathbf{2} = \mathbf{3}$ The prime factors for 24 are 2, 2, 2, and 3. $2 \bullet 2 \bullet 2 \bullet 3 = 24$ Note that 2 and 3 are divisible only by 1 and the numbers 2 or 3.

Example 2: Find the prime factors for 6. $6 \div 2 = 3$. The prime factors for 6 are 2 and 3.

Example 3: Find the prime factors for 15. $15 \div \mathbf{2}$ does not equal a natural number. Try $15 \div \mathbf{3} = 5$. Five is divisible only by 5 or 1. The prime numbers for 15 are **5** and **3**.

Example 4: Find the prime factors for 90. $90 \div \mathbf{2} = 45$ $45 \div \mathbf{3} = 15$ $15 \div \mathbf{3} = \mathbf{5}$

Find the prime factors for each of the following numbers. List the prime factors on the blank.

1) 14 the prime factors are ________________________

2) 48 the prime factors are ________________________

3) 600 the prime factors are ________________________

4) 512 the prime factors are ________________________

5) 238 the prime factors are ________________________

6) 96 the prime factors are ________________________

7) 500 the prime factors are ________________________

Name ______________________________ Date ______________________________

Prime Factors and Simplifying Square Root Radicals (continued)

In addition to knowing how to find prime factors, you need to understand that when two similar square radicals are multiplied, the answer is that number itself.

Example 1: Find $\sqrt{4} \bullet \sqrt{4}$. $2 \bullet 2 = 4$ so $\sqrt{4} \bullet \sqrt{4} = 4$

Example 2: Find $\sqrt{2} \bullet \sqrt{2}$. $1.414213562 \bullet 1.414\,213562 = 2$ so $\sqrt{2} \bullet \sqrt{2} = 2$

Example 3: Find $2\sqrt{2} \bullet \sqrt{2}$. $2 \bullet 2 = 4$

Now you can use what you know about prime factors to simplify square root radicals.

Example 1: Simplify $\sqrt{18}$. The prime factors are $2 \bullet 3 \bullet 3$, so $\sqrt{18}$ can be rewritten as $\sqrt{2} \bullet \sqrt{3} \bullet \sqrt{3}$.

Simplify $\sqrt{18}$. $\sqrt{2} \bullet \sqrt{3} \bullet \sqrt{3} = \sqrt{2} \bullet 3 = 3\sqrt{2} = 3 \bullet 1.414213542 = 4.242640686$
$\sqrt{18} = 4.242640686$

Simplify the following square root radicals. List the prime factors on blank a), and simplify the problem on blank b). The first one has been completed.

8) $\sqrt{12}$ = a) 2, 2, 3 b) $\sqrt{2} \bullet \sqrt{2} \bullet \sqrt{3} = 2\sqrt{3} = 3.464101615$

9) $\sqrt{63}$ = a) ______________ b) ______________________________

10) $2\sqrt{12}$ = a) ______________ b) ______________________________

11) $\sqrt{54}$ = a) ______________ b) ______________________________

12) $\sqrt{12} + \sqrt{18}$ = prime factors of $\sqrt{12}$ a) ______________________________

$\sqrt{12}$ simplified b) ______________________________

the prime factors of $\sqrt{18}$ c) ______________________________

$\sqrt{18}$ simplified d) ______________________________

The simplified $\sqrt{12} + \sqrt{18}$ = e) _____ + _____ = _______

Name ______________________ Date ______________________

RATIONALIZING THE DENOMINATORS IN RADICALS WITH FRACTIONS

In many problems fractions and radicals will appear together. Many fractions with radicals can be simplified by finding the roots of the numerator and denominator.

Examples: $\frac{\sqrt{4}}{\sqrt{9}} = \frac{2}{3}$ or $\frac{\sqrt{16}}{\sqrt{49}} = \frac{4}{7}$

In the examples above, each of the roots resulted in a rational number. Many times the fraction under the radical contains a denominator that is an irrational number.

Example: In $\frac{\sqrt{4}}{\sqrt{7}}$ the square root of seven is an irrational number.

To rationalize the denominator, the fraction is changed so the denominator does not have a radical.

Example: To rationalize $\frac{\sqrt{4}}{\sqrt{7}}$, it is necessary to find a number that can be multiplied times $\sqrt{7}$ and result in a rational number. You have learned that $\sqrt{7} \bullet \sqrt{7} = 7$. Seven is a rational number. If the denominator is multiplied by $\sqrt{7}$ the numerator must be multiplied by $\sqrt{7}$.

To rationalize the denominator of $\frac{\sqrt{4}}{\sqrt{7}}$ the numerator and denominator must both be multiplied by $\sqrt{7}$.

$$\frac{\sqrt{4}}{\sqrt{7}} \bullet \frac{\sqrt{7}}{\sqrt{7}} = \frac{\sqrt{28}}{7}$$

A radical is in simplified form when the radicand has no roots other than 1. The radical $\frac{\sqrt{28}}{7}$ must be simplified because $\sqrt{28} = \sqrt{4} \bullet \sqrt{7}$. Seven has no roots other than 7 and 1. However, the root of 4 is 2.

Simplified: $\frac{\sqrt{28}}{7} = \sqrt{4} \bullet \frac{\sqrt{7}}{7} = \frac{2\sqrt{7}}{7}$

Simplify the following. Show all steps.

1) $\frac{\sqrt{4}}{\sqrt{5}} =$

2) $\frac{\sqrt{2}}{\sqrt{3}} =$

3) $\frac{\sqrt{3}}{\sqrt{6}} =$

4) $\frac{\sqrt{50}}{\sqrt{2}} =$

5) $\frac{\sqrt{8}}{\sqrt{2}} =$

Name ______________________ Date ______________________

Learning about Radicals in Equations

Radicals often occur in equations. An **equation** states that two numbers or algebraic expressions are equal. When a radical appears in an equation, a variable (unknown) appears as the radicand. Variables are letters, sometimes called literal numbers, used to represent numbers. Any letter *a* through *z* may be used as a variable.

Example1: $\sqrt{x} = 2$ is an equation with a radical. The radicand is a variable (x).

To solve equations like $\sqrt{x} = 2$ use the following steps.

Step 1: Square each side of the equation: $\sqrt{x} \bullet \sqrt{x} = 2 \bullet 2$ results in $x = 4$
Step 2: Substitute 4 in the original equation and solve the equation.
$\sqrt{4} = 2$. The square root of 4 is 2.
Step 3: Rewrite the equation with 2 replacing $\sqrt{4}$. $2 = 2$

Solve the following. In blank a) show the radical side of the equation squared, in blank b) show the other side of the equation squared, in c) indicate what the variable equals, in d) rewrite the equation replacing the variable, and in e) rewrite the solved equation. The first one has been completed.

1) $\sqrt{x} = 3$ a) $\sqrt{x} \bullet \sqrt{x}$ b) $3 \bullet 3$ c) $x = 9$ d) $\sqrt{9} = 3$ e) $3 = 3$

2) $\sqrt{x} = 4$ a) ________ b) ________ c) ________ d) ________ e) ________

3) $\sqrt{x} = 9$ a) ________ b) ________ c) ________ d) ________ e) ________

4) $\sqrt{x} = 5$ a) ________ b) ________ c) ________ d) ________ e) ________

5) $\sqrt{x} = 6$ a) ________ b) ________ c) ________ d) ________ e) ________

6) $\sqrt{x} = 7$ a) ________ b) ________ c) ________ d) ________ e) ________

7) $\sqrt{x} = 8$ a) ________ b) ________ c) ________ d) ________ e) ________

8) $\sqrt{x} = 12$ a) ________ b) ________ c) ________ d) ________ e) ________

9) $\sqrt{x} = 15$ a) ________ b) ________ c) ________ d) ________ e) ________

10) $\sqrt{x} = 10$ a) ________ b) ________ c) ________ d) ________ e) ________

Name ______________________ Date ______________________

Quiz VIII: Learning About Radicals and Roots

Draw a radical for each of the following statements.

1) The square root of forty-nine. __________

2) The fourth root of sixty-four. __________

3) The cube root of one hundred twenty-five. __________

4) The eighth root of two hundred fifty-six. __________

Write the statement that expresses each of the following.

5) $\sqrt{8}$ ______________________________

6) $\sqrt[3]{8}$ ______________________________

7) $\sqrt[6]{78}$ ______________________________

Find the indicated root of each radical and write the root on blank a). Write the factors on blank b).

8) $\sqrt{81}$ = a) ________ b) ________ 9) $\sqrt[4]{16}$ = a) ________ b) ________

10) $\sqrt[3]{27}$ = a) ________ b) ________ 11) $\sqrt[5]{32}$ = a) ________ b) ________

Multiply the following radicals

12) $\sqrt{7} \bullet \sqrt{2} =$ ________ 13) $\sqrt{7} \bullet \sqrt{5} =$ ________ 14) $\sqrt{3} \bullet 2\sqrt{6} =$ ________

Divide the following.

15) $\sqrt{6} \div \sqrt{2} =$ ________ 16) $\sqrt{24} \div \sqrt{8} =$ ________ 17) $\sqrt{49} \div \sqrt{7} =$ ________

Simplify the following.

18) $\sqrt{12} =$ ______________ 19) $5\sqrt{18} =$ ______________

20) $\dfrac{\sqrt{3}}{\sqrt{4}} =$ ______________ 21) $\dfrac{\sqrt{2}}{\sqrt{3}} =$ ______________

Complete the following blanks.

22) Radicals can be added if the __________ and the __________ are the same.

23) Tell why the radicals $2\sqrt{12}$ and $3\sqrt{12}$ can be added. ______________

24) Radicals can be subtracted if the __________ and the __________ are the same.

25) Tell why the radical $3\sqrt{12}$ cannot be subtracted from $2\sqrt{2}$. ______________

____

Name ______________________________ Date ______________________________

Learning About Linear Equations

Linear equations are **first degree** equations. The graph of a linear equation is a straight line.

There are two requirements for an equation to be a first degree equation.

1. In a first degree equation, each of the **variables** has an exponent of 1.
   For example: x, y, and z all have exponents of 1, but x^2, y^3, z^4 all have exponents greater than 1.
2. Two variables do not appear as a **product** in any term.
   For example: x, y, and, z are individual variables, but xy, xz, and yz are examples of variables appearing as a product.
   If $x = 4$ and $y = 2$, then $xy = 4 \bullet 2 = 8$.

Example: $x + y = 10$ The variables are x and y, and each has the exponent 1.
$3x - 2y = 11$ The variables are x and y, and each has the exponent 1.
$x^3 + y^2 = 17$ The variables x and y each have exponents greater than 1.

Example: $x + y = 10$ The variables do not appear as a product in any term.
$2xy + 5 = 27$ The variables x and y appear as a product.
If $x = 4$ and $y = 3$, then $2xy + 5 = 27$ equals $2 \bullet 4 \bullet 3 + 5 = 29$

Place a (+) in front of each of the following that is a **first degree** equation.

_____ 1) $xy = 36$ _____ 2) $x - y = 7$

_____ 3) $y = x + 14$ _____ 4) $xy - z = 8$

_____ 5) $x + y - z = 10$ _____ 6) $3x = 15$

_____ 7) $2x + y = 15$ _____ 8) $x^3 + y = 12$

_____ 9) $x + y^4 = 19$ _____ 10) $xy - z^2 = 16$

Name ______________________________ Date ______________________________

Determining the Slope of a Graphed Linear Equation

Graphing linear equations always results in a straight line. If you locate the coordinates for two points and connect them with a straight line, the other coordinates that lie on the line will also be solutions to the equation.

The following coordinate system has graphs of the linear equations $y = 3x$, $y = x$, and $y = -2x$.

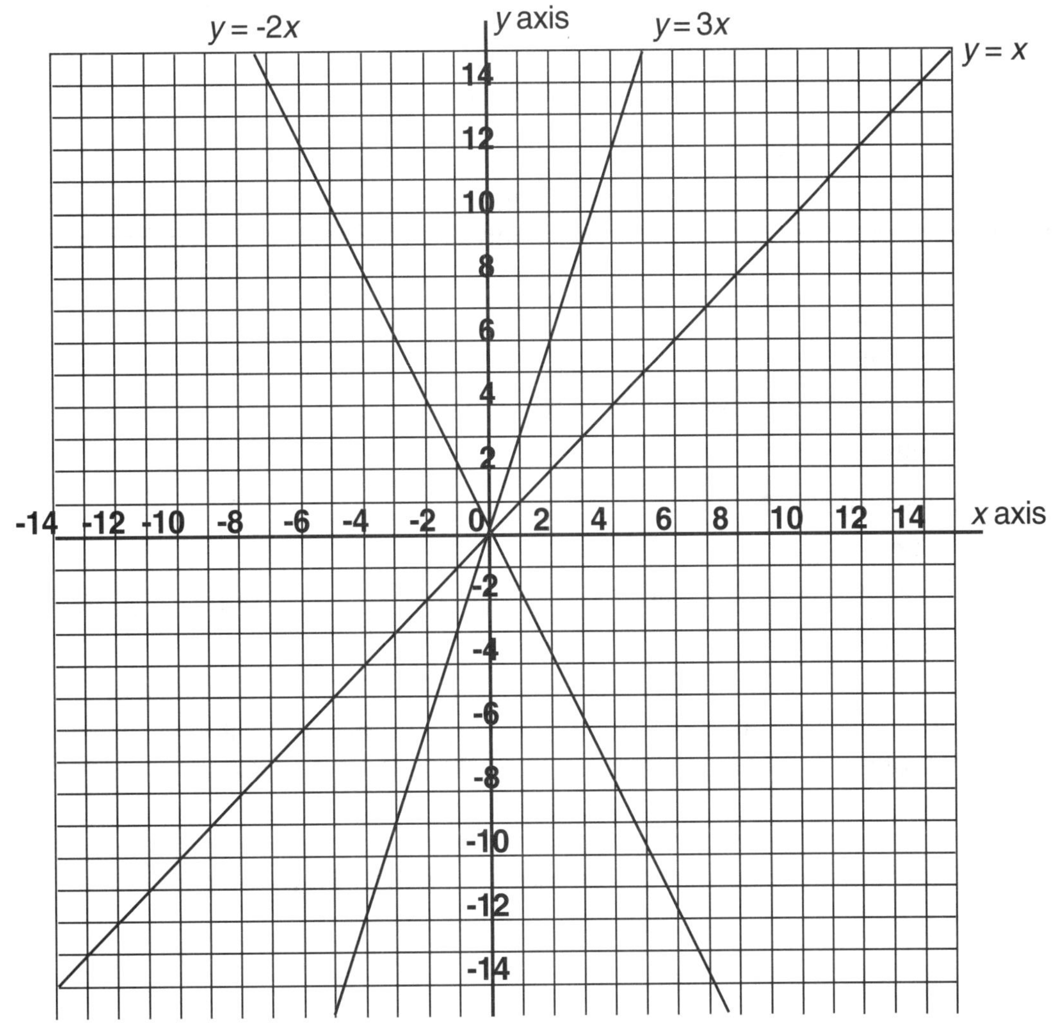

Fill in the following. Select your answers from: **linear; straight; first; x; y; and 0,0**.

1) The graphs of all three equations are ______________ lines.
2) All three of the equations are of the ________ degree.
3) All three of the equations are ___________ equations.
4) All three graphs cross the "___" and "___" axis at the coordinates ___, ___.

Name ______________________________ Date ______________________________

Determining the Slope of a Graphed Linear Equation (continued)

The graph of a linear equation may be referred to as **positive** or **negative.** To determine if a graph is positive or negative, the **slope** of the graph must be determined. In determining the slope, the graph is read from left to right to determine if the graph slopes up or down. See "A" and "B" below.

A. Positive Slope

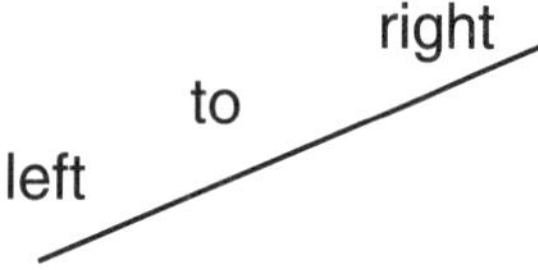

B. Negative Slope

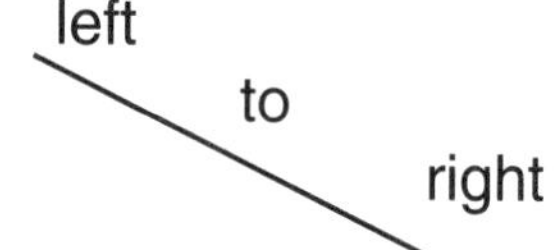

Graph A above is a positive-sloping graph since the line slopes up when read from left to right. Graph B is a negative-sloping graph since the line slopes down when read from left to right.

Answer the following questions:

5) The graph of the linear equation $y = 3x$ slopes ________ from left to ________ and is a ________ sloping graph.

6) The graph of the linear equation $y = x$ slopes ________ from ________ to right and is a ________ sloping graph.

7) The graph of the linear equation $y = -2x$ slopes ________ from ________ to right and is a ________ sloping graph.

Making a table of values for the x and y coordinates that are solutions to the equation is helpful. In making a table, numerical values are chosen and assigned to x. Then the equation is solved for y, and the numerical values are placed in table format.

Develop numerical values for the linear equations $y = 3x$ and $y = -3x$ and place the values in the tables below.

$y = 3x$

If x =				
Then y =				

$y = -3x$

If x =				
Then y =				

Name ______________________________ Date ______________________________

Determining the Slope of a Graphed Linear Equation (continued)

Use the numerical values from the tables on the previous page to graph the equations $y = 3x$ and $y = -3x$ on the coordinate system below. For each pair of coordinates, the x coordinate is written first and the y coordinate is written second. Find the x coordinate on the grid by moving along the x axis. Then move up or down on the line of the x coordinate until you find the point where it intersects the line of the y coordinate. Mark that point with a dot and then continue to find the other points from the table. Connect the dots for each equation with a straight line.

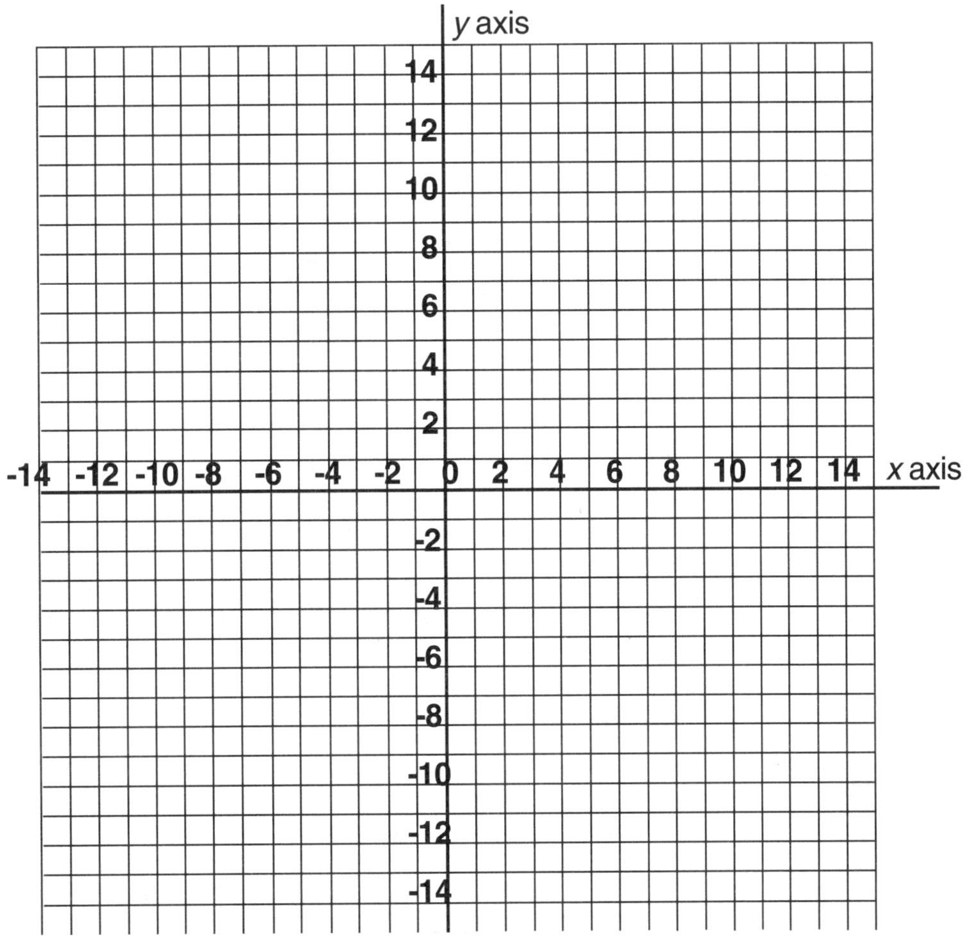

Answer the following questions.

8) The equation __ = ___ is a positive-sloping graph because when read ___________

____

9) The equation __ = ___ is a negative-sloping graph because when read ___________

____

Name ______________________ Date ______________________

Positive and Negative Slope

It is important to determine if the slope of a graph is positive or negative as well as how **steep** the slope of the line is. In order to determine how steep the slope of a line is, one needs to determine how much *y* changes with each change in *x*. Refer to the graph of the linear equation $y = 3x$ on the coordinate system below. Answer the following questions.

1) In determining the slope of the line, one must read the line from
   a) right to left b) left to right.
2) The slope of the line $y = 3x$ is (up/down).
3) The slope of the line is (negative/positive).

You will note that the graph of $y = 3x$ on the coordinate system below has dashed lines (- -) marked a-f. Refer to this dashed line and answer the following questions.

4) In moving from "a" to "b," one moves a) 1 b) 2 c)3 d) 4 places on the *x* line.
5) In moving from "b" to "c," one moves a) 1 b) 2 c)3 d) 4 places on the *y* line.
6) In moving from "c" to "d," one moves a) 1 b) 2 c)3 d) 4 places on the *x* line.
7) In moving from "d" to "e," one moves a) 1 b) 2 c)3 d) 4 places on the *y* line.
8) In moving from "e" to "f," one moves a) 1 b) 2 c)3 d) 4 places on the *x* line.
9) In the graph of $y = 3x$, each time the *x* position changed by a)1 b)2 c)3 d)4.
10) In the graph of $y = 3x$, each time the *y* position changed by a)1 b)2 c)3 d)4.
11) In the graph of $y = 3x$, the change in *y* is a) 3 b)1 c)5 d) 10 times the change in *x*.
12) In the graph of $y = 3x$, the change in *x* is a) 1/5 b) 1/3 c) 1/10 d) 1/100 of the change in *y*.

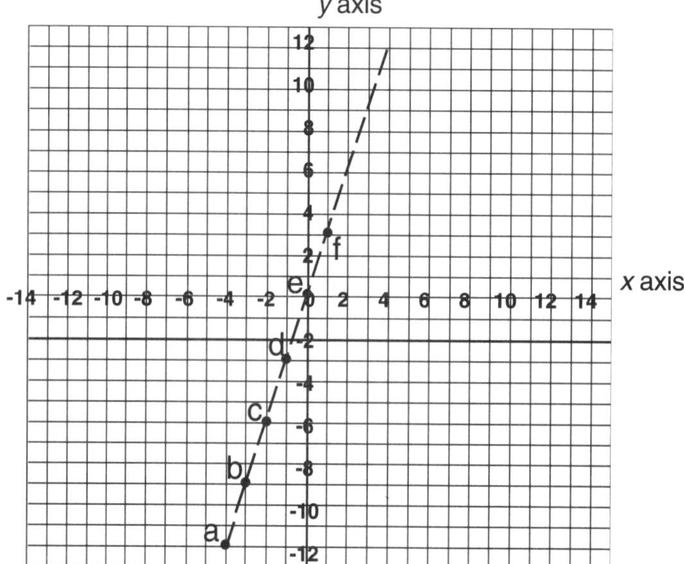

Name ______________________________ Date ______________________________

Formula for Determining the Slope of a Graphed Linear Equation

The following formula is used in determining the slope of the graph of a linear equation.

$$\text{Slope} = \frac{y_2 - y_1}{x_2 - x_1}$$

The solution of the equation requires any two y (y_2,y_1) coordinates and any two x (x_2,x_1) coordinates from the same sets of coordinates or graph.

The following coordinates for the linear equation $y = 3x$ can be used to demonstrate the above formula. The coordinates are (1,3) (2,6) (0,0) (-1,-3). Remember the first number in each set of coordinates is the x coordinate, and the second number in the set is the y coordinate.

Example: Use the formula $\text{Slope} = \frac{y_2 - y_1}{x_2 - x_1}$ and the above coordinates of the graph $y = 3x$ to find the slope of the graph. Substitute the coordinates sets of (1,3) and (2,6) in the above formula to determine the slope of the linear equation $y = 3x$.

$\text{Slope} = \frac{6 - 3}{2 - 1} = \frac{3}{1} = 3$ The slope of the linear equation $y = 3x$ is 3.

Refer again to the graph of the equation $y = 3x$ on page 70 and complete the following exercise.

1) Place a plus (+) by the sets of coordinates that lie on the graph for the linear equation $y = 3x$.
__ a) 3,9 __ b)2,2 __ c) -2,-6 __ d) 7,21 __ e) -4,-12 __ f) 5,15

2) Plot the coordinates for Question 1 that lie on the graph $y = 3x$, and draw a line connecting the coordinates to the graph.

Name ______________________________ Date ______________________________

Graphing Linear Equations and Determining Their Slopes

Determine a table of values for the following linear equations and plot the points on the coordinate system below. Draw lines to graph the sets of coordinates.

1) $y = 2x + 1$

2) $y = 2x - 1$

3) $y = -2x + 1$

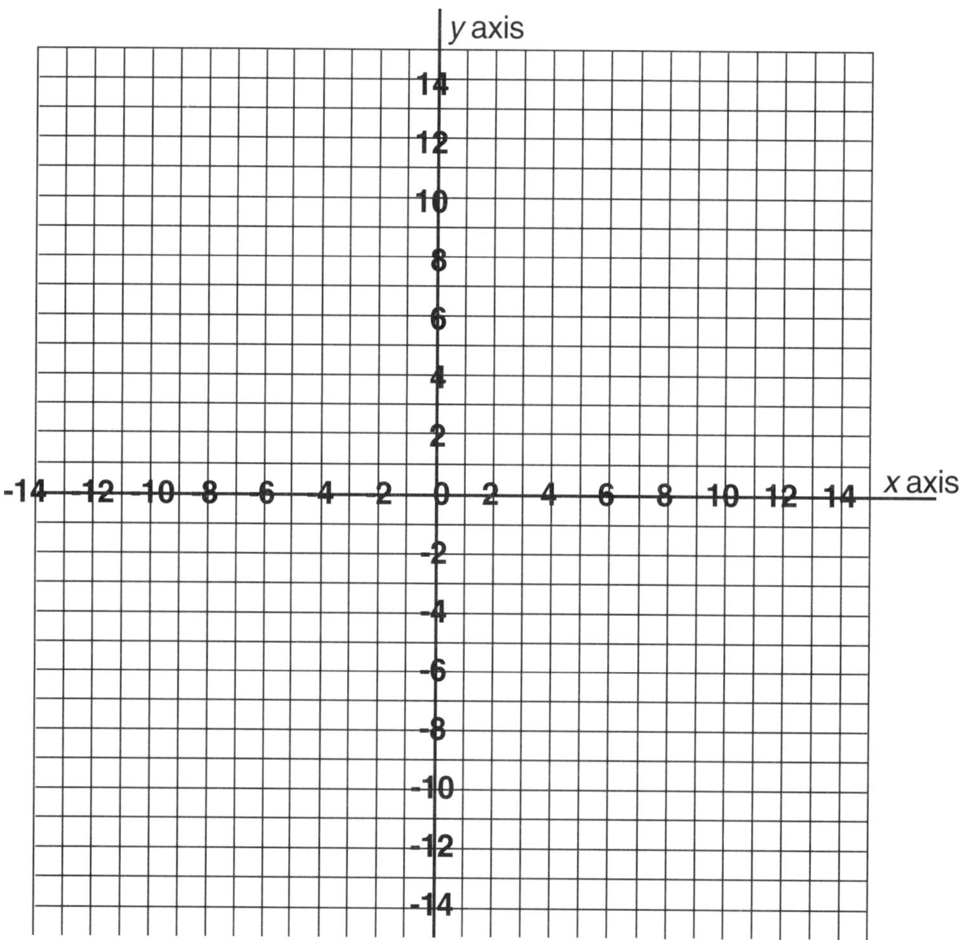

Name ______________________________ Date ______________________________

Graphing Linear Equations and Determining Their Slopes (continued)

Refer to the graphs for $y = 2x + 1$, $y = 2x - 1$, and $y = -2x + 1$, and answer the following questions.

Linear equation $y = 2x + 1$

4) The slope of the linear equation $y = 2x + 1$ is (negative/positive).

5) Coordinates for the linear equation $y = 2x + 1$ are ____ , ____, ____, ____ , ____.

6) Choose four sets of two coordinates for $y = 2x + 1$, and complete the formula below. Determine the slope of the graph.

Slope = ________ = ______ = Slope = ________ = ______ =

Slope = ________ = ______ = Slope = ________ = ______ =

7) The slope of the linear equation $y = 2x + 1$ is____ .

Linear equation $y = 2x - 1$

8) The slope of the linear equation $y = 2x - 1$ is (negative/positive).

9) Coordinates for the linear equation $y = 2x - 1$ are ____ ,____,____, ____ , ____.

10) Complete the following formulas and determine the steepness of the slope.

Slope = ________ = ______ = Slope = ________ = ______ =

Slope = ________ = ______ = Slope = ________ = ______ =

11) The slope of the linear equation $y = 2x - 1$ is ____.

Linear equation $y = -2x + 1$

12) The slope of the linear equation $y = -2x + 1$ is (negative/positive).

13) Coordinates for the linear equation $y = -2x + 1$ are ____, ____,____, ____, ____.

14) Complete the following formulas and determine the steepness of the slope.

Slope = ________ = ______ = Slope = ________ = ______ =

Slope = ________ = ______ = Slope = ________ = ______ =

15) The slope of the linear equation $y = -2x + 1$ is ____.

Name ______________________________ Date ______________________________

Learning About the *x*-Intercept and *y*-Intercept

The coordinates where the graph of a linear equation crosses the x axis and y axis are important coordinates. In algebra these coordinates are known as the x-intercept and y-intercept. To begin learning about the x- and y-intercepts, graph the following linear equations on the coordinate system below. Plot the coordinates following each equation.

A. $y = 3x + 2$ (0,2) (-1,-1) (1,5)

B. $y = 3x - 2$ (0,-2) (2,4) (-1,-5)

C. $y = x + 5$ (0,5) (-5,0) (3,8)

D. $y = -x - 5$ (0,-5) (-5,0) (-8,3)

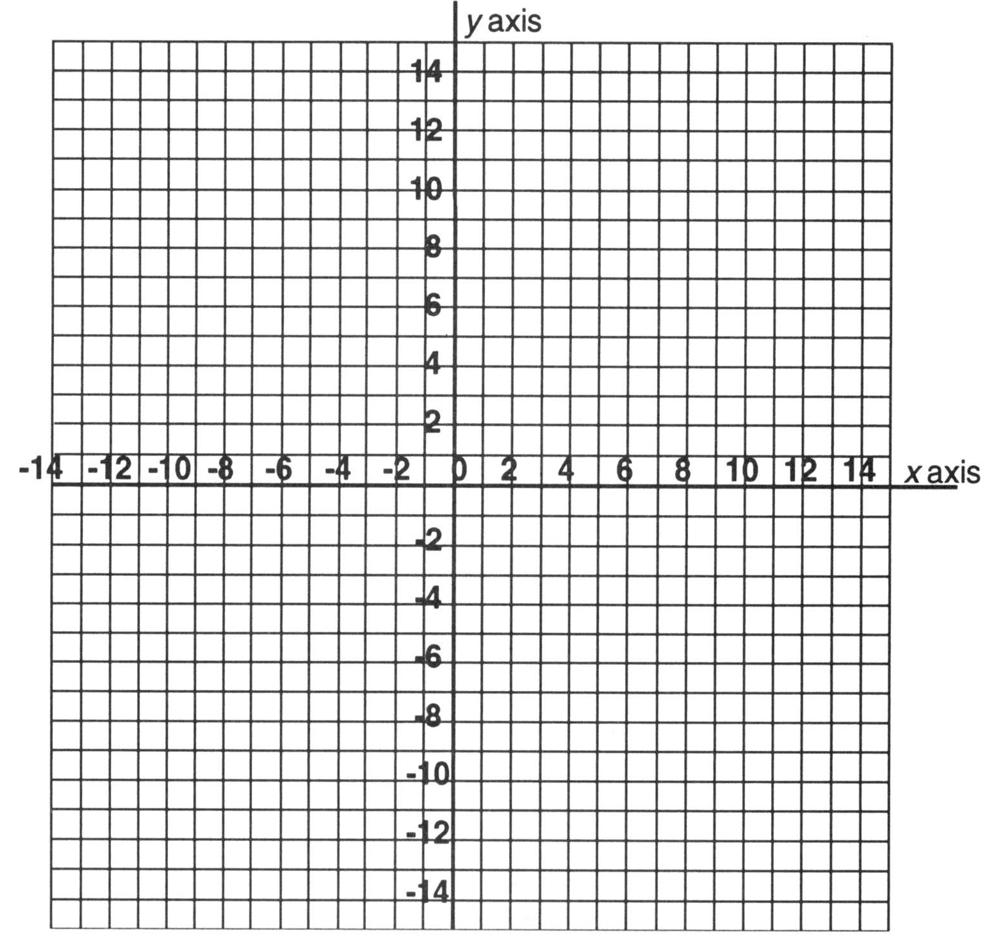

Refer to the above graphs and answer the following questions.

1) List the linear equations for the graph(s) with a positive slope.

____

2) List the linear equations for the graph(s) with a negative slope.

____

3) The linear equation $y = 3x + 2$ crosses the y-axis at the **coordinates** ___, ___.

Name ______________________________ Date ______________________________

Learning About the x-Intercept and y-Intercept (continued)

4) The point where the graph of $y = 3x + 2$ crosses the y-axis is the ***y*-intercept**.

   The **coordinates** for the y-intercept are ___ , ___.

5) The point where the graph of $y = 3x + 2$ crosses the x-axis is the ***x*-intercept**.

   The **coordinates** for the x-intercept are ___ , ___.

6) The linear equation $y = 3x + 2$ crosses the x-axis at the **coordinates** ___ , ___.

7) The coordinates for the ***x*-intercept** for the linear equation $y = 3x - 2$ are ___ , ___.

8) The coordinates for the ***y*-intercept** for the linear equation $y = 3x - 2$ are ___ , ___.

9) The coordinates for the ***x*-intercept** for the linear equation $y = x + 5$ are ___ , ___.

10) The coordinates for the ***y*-intercept** for the linear equation $y = x + 5$ are ___ , ___.

11) The coordinates for the ***x*-intercept** for the linear equation $y = -x - 5$ are ___ , ___.

12) The coordinates for the ***y*-intercept** for the linear equation $y = -x - 5$ are ___ , ___.

13) In locating the ***x*-intercept** the y coordinate will always be a) 6 b) 10 c) 0 d) 9

14) In locating the ***y*-intercept** the x coordinate will always be a) 6 b) 10 c) 0 d) 9

Solve the following equations

15) $y = 4x - 4$ (let x equal zero) $y = 4(\_\_) - 4$ $y =$ ___ $= y$-intercept

16) $y = 4x - 4$ (let y equal zero) $0 = 4(\_\_) - 4$ $x =$ ___ $= x$-intercept

17) $y = x + 2$ (let x equal zero) $y = (\_\_) + 2$ $y =$ ___ $= y$-intercept

18) $y = x + 2$ (let y equal zero) $0 = (\_\_) + 2$ $x =$ ___ $= x$-intercept

19) In solving the above equations to find the y-intercept, x equals _____ .

20) In solving the above equations to find the x-intercept, y equals _____ .

Name ______________________ Date ______________________

Learning About the Slope Intercept Equation

Graphing linear equations to find the solution to an equation is an important problem-solving method. The equation $y = mx + b$ is valuable in the study of mathematics. This equation is called the **slope intercept equation**. To find the slope and y-intercept of a linear equation, the equation must be written in the form $y = mx + b$. It is important to note that the **slope** is the **ratio** of **vertical change** compared to the **horizontal change** in the graph.

In solving linear equations using the slope intercept equation, it is often necessary to rewrite the equation so that it is in the form $y = mx + b$.

Example: Rewrite the equation $3x - y = 8$ so that it is in the form $y = mx + b$.

Step 1: Add $(+y)$ to each member: $3x - y + y = 8 + y$ equals $3x = 8 + y$

Step 2: Subtract (-8) from each member: $3x - 8 = -8 + 8 + y$ equals $3x - 8 = y$

Step 3: $3x - 8 = y$ can be rewritten in the $y = mx + b$ form as $y = 3x - 8$

$y = 3x - 8$ is in the slope intercept form

Step 4: Develop a table of values for the equation.

For example:

x	-2	-1	1	2	3	4
y	-14	-11	-5	-2	1	4

Step 5: Plot the graph for the coordinates in step 4.

The next exercise will help determine the slope of the equation $3x - y = 8$ which can be rewritten in the form $y = mx + b$ as $y = 3x - 8$. You will recall that the slope is the ratio of the vertical change in the graph compared to the horizontal change in the graph.

Use a colored pencil and complete the following on the graph on the next page.

1) Place a dot locating the coordinates (-2,-14).
2) Place a dot locating the coordinates (-1,-11).
3) On the x line draw a **horizontal** line from -2 to -1.
4) On the y line draw a **vertical** line from -14 to -11.
5) The **horizontal** line change is a) 5 b)6 c)1 d)9 units.
6) The **vertical** line change is a) 3 b) 8 c) 7 d) 6 units.
7) The ratio of vertical change to horizontal is a) 3/1 b) 4/1 c) 5/1 d)6/1.
8) Place a dot locating the coordinates (1,-5).
9) Place a dot locating the coordinates (2,-2).
10) On the x line draw a **horizontal** line from 1 to 2.
11) On the y line draw a **vertical** line from -5 to -2.
12) The **horizontal** line change is a) 1 b)5 c)6 d)9 units.
13) The **vertical** line change is a) 7 b) 8 c)3 d)6 units.
14) The ratio of vertical change to horizontal is a) 4/1 b) 5/1 c) 3/1 d) 6/1.

Name ________________________________ Date ____________________________

Learning About the Slope Intercept Equation (continued)

15) Place a dot locating the coordinates (3,1).
16) Place a dot locating the coordinates (4,4).
17) On the x line draw a **horizontal** line from 3 to 4.
18) On the y line draw a **vertical** line from 1 to 4.
19) The **horizontal** line change is a) 9 b)5 c)6 d)1 units.
20) The **vertical** line change is a) 7 b) 3 c)8 d)6 units.
21) The ratio of vertical change to horizontal is a) 4/1 b) 6/1 c) 5/1 d) 3/1.
22) In the linear equation $y = 3x - 8$ the ratio of vertical change to horizontal change is ____ /____ or ___.

Compare the equations $y = 3x - 8$ and the $y = mx + b$ and answer the following questions.

23) In the equation $y = 3x - 8$, the number ____ replaces "m."
24) In the equation $y = 3x - 8$, the number ____ replaces "b."

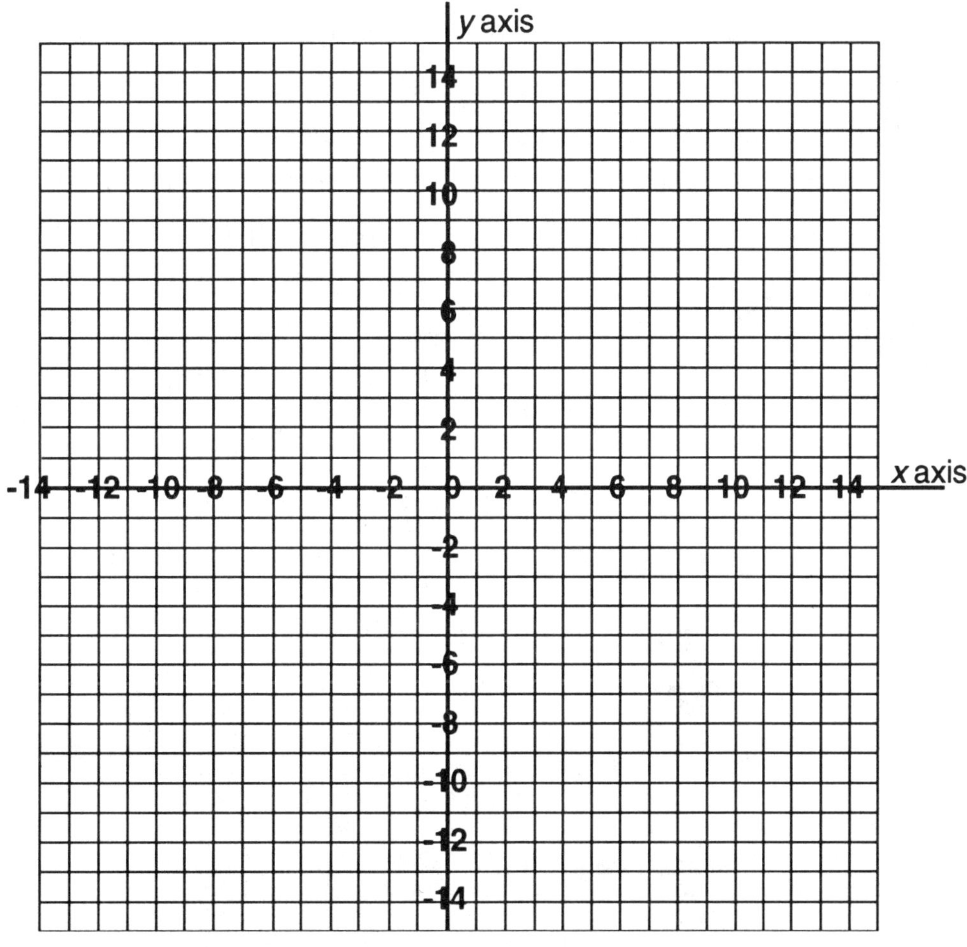

Name ______________________________ Date ______________________________

Slope Intercept Exercises

In the slope intercept equation $y = mx + b$, the number replacing the letter m will always give the **slope** of the equation. The number that replaces the letter b will always be the ***y*-intercept**. Therefore, it is important to write a linear equation in the form $y = mx + b$.

Write the following equations in the slope/intercept form.

1) $y - 1 = 2x$ ______________________ 2) $y - 2x = 8$ ______________________

3) $y - 7 = x$ ______________________ 4) $3y - x = 2$ ______________________

Give the slope and y-intercept for each of the following linear equations

5) $y = 4x + 5$ a) slope ___ /___ b) y-intercept _____

6) $y = \frac{1}{2}x - 2$ a) slope ___ /___ b) y-intercept _____

7) $y = x + 1$ a) slope ___ /___ b) y-intercept _____

8) $y - 1 = x$ a) slope ___ /___ b) y-intercept _____

Refer to the **slope intercept equation** $y = mx + b$, and place a plus (+) by the true statements.

_____ 9) In the slope intercept equation m indicates the slope of the line.

_____ 10) In the slope intercept equation b locates the y-intercept.

_____ 11) In the slope intercept equation y is the independent variable.

_____ 12) In the slope intercept equation x is the dependent variable.

Refer to the graph below and answer the following questions.

13) The graph intercepts (crosses) the y-axis at a) +9 b) +8 c) +1 d) -5

14) The graph has a (negative/positive) slope.

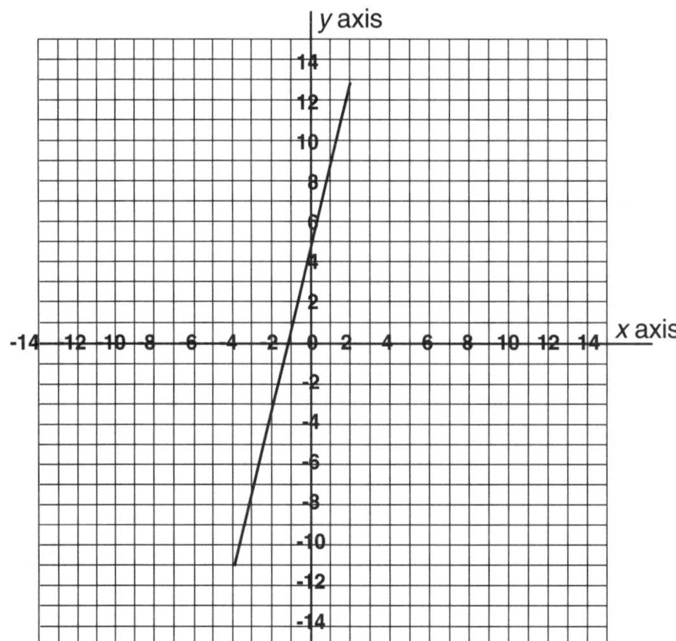

Name ______________________ Date ______________________

Graphing Linear Equations

In the next exercise you will graph two linear equations on the same coordinate plane. Find two sets of coordinates that are solutions for each of the linear equations, locate the coordinates, and draw a graph of each linear equation.

Graph the linear equations $x + y = 8$ and $x - y = 4$.

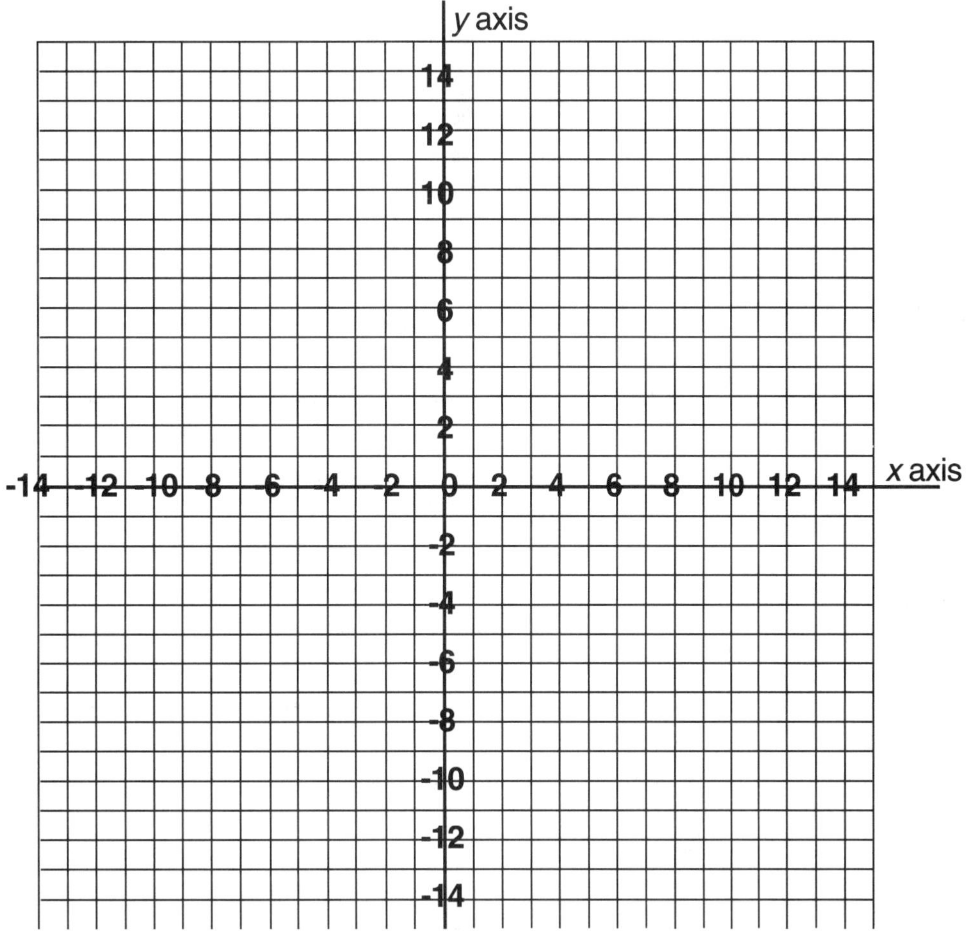

Refer to the graphs of $x + y = 8$ and $x - y = 4$, and answer the following questions.

1) The coordinates where the graphs cross are a) 5,1 b) 6,2 c) -3,0 d) 6,8

2) Substitute the coordinates where the graphs cross into each of the equations $x + y = 8$ and $x - y = 4$, and solve the equations.

   a) x + y = 8 ______________ b) x - y = 4 ______________

3) The coordinates a) (__ ,__) where the graphs cross are solutions for both b) ___ + ___ = 8 and c) ___ - ___ = 4.

Name ______________________ Date ______________________

Reviewing What You Have Learned

In the following exercise, place a plus (+) on the blank that describes the characteristics of the expression shown. For example, if the expression is a monomial, place a + opposite that expression under that column. In the sixth blank, place a + if the expression is a first degree expression. In the last blank, place a + if the expression is an algebraic expression.

	polynomial	monomial	binomial	trinomial	linear	first degree	algebraic
1) $x + y$	___	___	___	___	___	___	___
2) $x - y + 3$	___	___	___	___	___	___	___
3) 4^2	___	___	___	___	___	___	___
4) $a^2 + b + c$	___	___	___	___	___	___	___
5) $2x^2 - 3y + 5$	___	___	___	___	___	___	___
6) $3^2x^3y^2$	___	___	___	___	___	___	___
7) x^3	___	___	___	___	___	___	___
8) $\frac{1}{2}x + 5y - z$	___	___	___	___	___	___	___
9) $\frac{2}{3}x^3 + 7$	___	___	___	___	___	___	___
10) $\frac{2}{3}x + y$	___	___	___	___	___	___	___
11) $5a^3b^2 - y^2 + 4$	___	___	___	___	___	___	___
12) $5s^2y^2x^3$	___	___	___	___	___	___	___
13) $\frac{1}{4}$	___	___	___	___	___	___	___
14) $7x - 9y$	___	___	___	___	___	___	___
15) $t^3y^2a^3 - 2xb + 144$	___	___	___	___	___	___	___

Name ______________________________ Date ______________________________

Quiz IX: Learning About Linear Equations

Fill in the following blanks. Select answers from the list below.

positive	**horizontal**	**one**	**linear equation**	$y = mx + b$	**down**
vertical	**left**	**first degree**	**negative**	**right**	**up**
$y = 2x + 4$	**ten**	$y = -2x + 4$	**m**	**numerator**	**two**
b	**denominator**				

An equation in the form $y = 3x - 8$ is known as a (1) _________ _________ . The variables in a linear equation all have an exponent of (2) ____ . When a linear equation is graphed, the slope of the graph may be (3) _________ or (4) _________ . The graph of a positive-sloping linear equation slopes (5) ________ from left to right. The graph of a negative-sloping linear equation slopes (6) ________ from left to right.

The graph of the linear equation (7) ___ = ___ + ___ will slope down. It is a (8) __________ -sloping graph. The graph of the linear equation (9) ___ = ___ + ___ will slope up. It is a (10) __________ -sloping graph.

The slope intercept equation is (11) ___ = ___ + ___. In the slope intercept equation, the number replacing the letter (12) ___ will always indicate the slope. The number replacing the letter (13) ___ will be the y-intercept. The slope of a graph is the ratio of the (14) ____________ change compared to the (15) ___________ change. The ratio of the slope is written as a fraction with the (16) ____________________ indicating the vertical change and the (17) _______________ indicating the horizontal change. The y-intercept of the graph for the linear equation $y = 2x + 10$ is (18) ___. The slope of the graph for the linear equation $y = 2x + 10$ is 19) ____.

Name ______________________________ Date ____________________________

Learning About Quadratic Equations

The **quadratic equation** is one of the most important algebraic tools. It is a second degree polynomial with one variable (unknown). In standard form it is written as the equation $ax^2 + bx + c = 0$

In the form $ax^2 + bx + c = 0$, the equation is written in descending power for the variable "x". To arrange in descending power of a variable, an equation is written from left to right with the variable descending in power.

Example: Arrange $x^3 + x^4 + (-2x) + 4x^5y$ in descending power of "x".

The term with x^5 is the highest power, so $4x^5y$ is the first term. The term with the second highest power is x^4, the third term is x^3, and so forth. Arranged in order from highest to lowest power in the variable "x," $x^3 + x^4 + (-2x) + 4x^5y$ becomes $4x^5y + x^4 + x^3 + (-2x)$.

Arrange the following in order from highest to lowest power for the variable indicated in parentheses.

1) $x^2 + x^5 + x^3 - y$ (x) = ___ + ___ + ___ - ___

2) $a^3 - a^2 + a^4$ (a) = ___ + ___ - ___

3) $5xy^3 - 4y^4 + y^2 - 2$ (y) = ______________________________

4) $5b^2 + b^4 - b^3 + 10b$ (b) = ______________________________

5) $x + x^2 - y$ (x) = ______________________________

6) $7t^2y^5 - t^4 + t^3x^2 + a^3t$ (t) = ______________________________

7) $q^3x^2 + 9q + 4y^5q^8$ (q) = ______________________________

8) $-2d + 6d^2r + d^9g^4$ (d) = ______________________________

9) $3r^5t - 4ar - 2a^4r^2 + r^8x$ (r) = ______________________________

10) $y^2x^4 + 6yt^2 + 2y - 8y^3b^2$ (y) = ______________________________

Name ______________________________ Date ______________________________

GRAPHING THE EQUATION $AX^2 + BX + C$

You have learned that the graph of a linear equation is a straight line. In learning about the graphs of quadratics, we will begin with $y = ax^2$. In the following activities you will graph sets of quadratic coordinates. You will find that each of the graphs results in a form known as a **parabola**. After graphing the different quadratics, you will be asked to determine one of the important characteristics of the parabola. Four equations will be graphed. Your teacher will give you two copies of the coordinate system on page 84. Place graph 1 and 2 on one coordinate system and graphs 3 and 4 on the other coordinate system.

Graph 1: $y = 1x^2$ The table of values is below. In this example $a = 1$.

x	0	1	2	3	-1	-2	-3
y	0	1	4	9	1	4	9

The coordinates of the graph will be (0,0), (1,1), (2,4), (3,9), (-1,1), (-2,4), and (-3,9). Plot the coordinates of the graph of $y = ax^2$ on the coordinate system on page 84. Connect the coordinates with a line.

Graph 2: $y = -2x^2$. The table of values is below. In this example $a = -2$.

x	0	1	2	3	-1	-2	-3
y	0	-2	-8	-18	-2	-8	-18

The coordinates of the graph will be (0,0), (1,-2), (2,-8), (3,-18), (-1,-2), (-2,-8), and (-3,-18). Plot the graph and connect the coordinates with a line.

Graph 3: $x = 1y^2$. The table of values is below. $a = 1$

y	0	1	2	3	-1	-2	-3
x	0	1	4	9	1	4	9

Plot the graph of $x = 1y^2$ on the coordinates and connect the coordinates with a line.

Graph 4: $x = -2y^2$ The table of values is below. $a = -2$

y	0	1	2	3	-1	-2	-3
x	0	-2	-8	-18	-2	-8	-18

Plot the graph of $x = -2y^2$ on the coordinates and connect the coordinates with a line.

Name ______________________________ Date ______________________________

Graphing the Equation $ax^2 + bx + c$ (continued)

Graph the quadratic equations from the previous page on the coordinate system below.

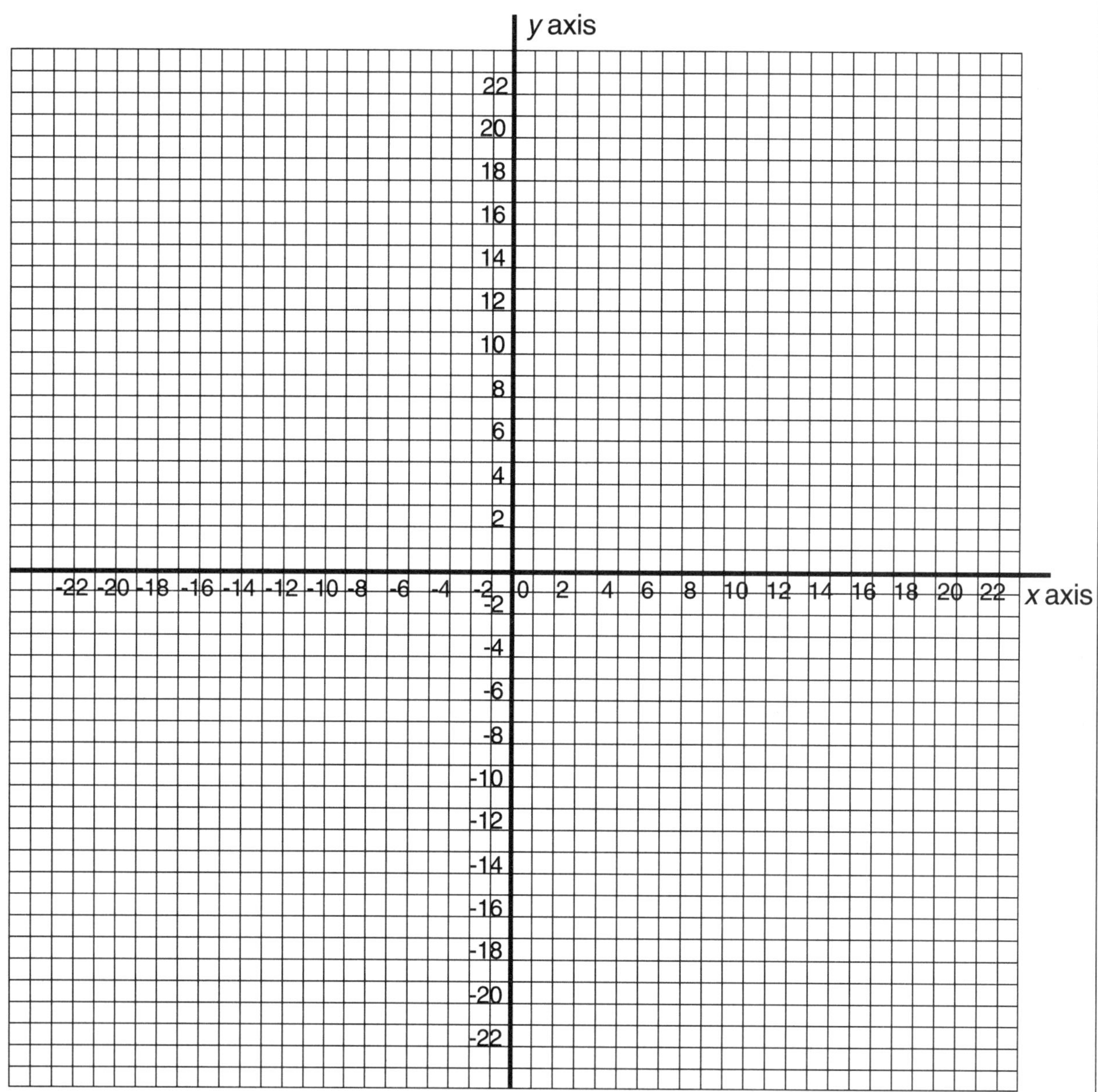

Name ______________________________ Date ____________________________

PARABOLAS

Each of the graphs you have drawn on page 84 is a **parabola**. In the study of parabolas, the terms **vertex**, **minimum coordinates**, and **maximum coordinates** are very important. Below you will find two parabolas marked "A" and "B". Use these parabolas to answer the following questions.

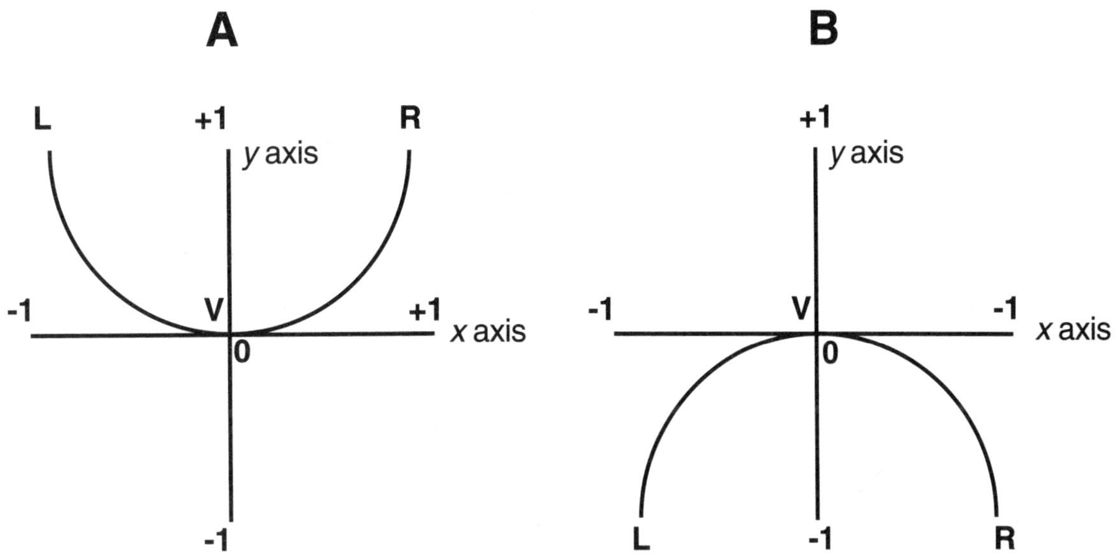

Refer to Parabola A and answer the following questions. Begin at Point **L** and follow the curve of the parabola to Point **V**.

1) The change in "y" as you move down the curve from Point L to Point V is from +____ to____.
2) From Point L to Point V the value of "y" is (decreasing/increasing).
3) The change in "x" as you move down the curve from Point L to Point V is from - ____ to____.
4) From Point L to Point V the value of "x" is (decreasing/increasing).

Refer to Parabola A and answer the following questions. Begin at Point **R** and follow the curve or the parabola to Point **V**.

5) The change in "y" as you move down the curve from Point R to Point V is from +____ to____.
6) From Point R to Point V the value of "y" is (decreasing/increasing).
7) The change in "x" as you move down the curve from Point R to Point V is from +____ to____.
8) From Point R to Point V the value of "x" is (decreasing/increasing).

Name ______________________________ Date ___________________________

Parabolas (continued)

Complete the following blanks using these terms: **maximum, minimum, vertex.**

On Parabola A, the coordinates of "x" and "y" reach their largest or (9)_________ values at Points L and R. The coordinates of "x" and "y" reach their smallest or (10) ___________ values at Point V. Point V is the (11) ________ value for Parabola A. Point V is the vertex of Parabola A.

Refer to Parabola B on the previous page and answer the following questions. Begin at Point L and follow the curve on the parabola to Point **V**.

12) The change in "y" as you move up the curve from Point L to Point V is from -__ to__.
13) From Point L to Point V the value of "y" is (decreasing/increasing).
14) The change in "x" as you move up the curve from Point L to Point V is from -__ to__.
15) From Point L to Point V the value of "x" is (decreasing/increasing).

Refer to Parabola B and answer the following questions. Begin at Point **R** and follow the curve on the parabola to Point **V**.

16) The change in "y" as you move up the curve from Point R to Point V is from -__ to__.
17) From Point R to Point V the value of "y" is (decreasing/increasing).
18) The change in "x" as you move up the curve from Point R to Point V is from +__ to__.
19) From Point R to Point V the value of "x" is (decreasing/increasing).

Complete the following blanks using the following terms: **maximum, minimum, vertex.**

On Parabola B, the coordinates of "x" and "y" reach their largest or (20) ________ values at Point V. The coordinates of "x" and "y" reach their smallest or (21) __________ values at Points L and R. Point V is the (23)________ value for Parabola B. Point V is the vertex of Parabola B.

Name ______________________________ Date ______________________________

Parabola Practice

$y = ax^2$

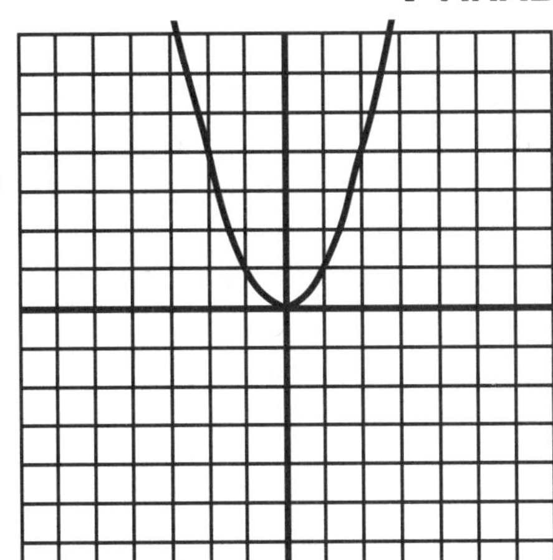

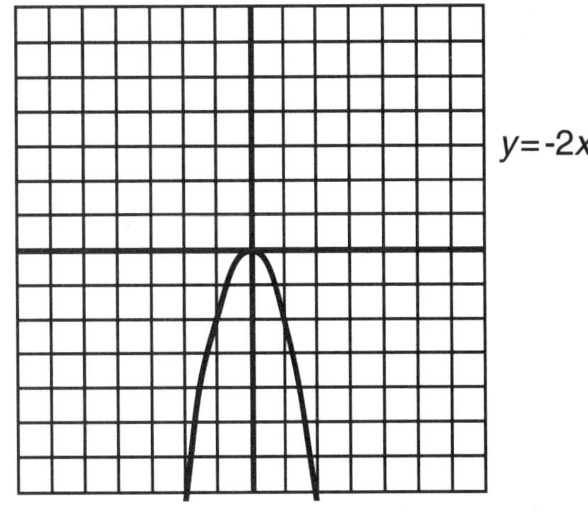

$y = -2x^2$

Refer to the parabola for $y = ax^2$, follow the instructions below, and answer the questions.

1) The minimum coordinates for the graph are a) 0,0 b) -1,-2 c) 1,1 d) -2,-2
2) Draw a line from (-1,1) through (0,1) to (1,1)
3) From (-1,1) to (0,1) the line is drawn through a) 1 b) 4 c) 7 d) 0 rectangles.
4) From (0,1) to (1,1) the line is drawn through a) 1 b) 4 c) 7 d) 0 rectangles.
5) Draw a line from (-2,3) through (0,3) to (2,3)
6) From (-2,3) to (0,3) the line is drawn through a) 1 b) 4 c) 7 d) 0 rectangles.
7) From (0,3) to (2,3) the line is drawn through a) 1 b) 4 c) 7 d) 0 rectangles.

Refer to the parabola for $y = -2x^2$, follow the instructions below, and answer the questions.

8) The maximum coordinates for the graph are a) 0,0 b) -1,-2 c) 1,1 d) -2,-2
9) Draw a line from (-1,-1) through (0,-1) to (1,-1)
10) From (-1,-1) to (0,-1) the line is drawn through a) 1 b) 4 c) 3 d) 0 rectangles.
11) From (0,-1) to (1,-1) the line is drawn through a) 1 b) 3 c) 7 d) 0 rectangles.
12) Draw a line from (-2,-2) through (0,-2) to (1,-2)
13) From (-2,-2) to (0,-2) the line is drawn through a) 1 b) 4 c) 7 d) 0 rectangles.
14) From (0,-2) to (+1,-2) the line is drawn through a) 1 b) 4 c) 7 d) 0 rectangles
15) Carefully fold the graphs for $y = ax^2$ and $y = -2x^2$ along the "y" axis.
16) Carefully fold the graphs for $x = ay^2$ and $x = -2y^2$ along the "x" axis.
17) When folded, the left and right sides of the graphs match exactly. (true/false)
18) The ("x"/ "y") axis divides the parabolas into two equal halves.
19) Define the word *symmetric:* ______________________________

Complete the following: Use the following terms.

$y = ax^2$ $y = -2x^2$ **symmetric** ***y* axis** **parabola** **(0,0)**

The graphs for $y = ax^2$ and $y = -2x^2$ are (20) __________ . Each of the graphs is a (21) __________ . The graph of (22) $y =$ _____ reaches its minimum point at the vertex. The graph of (23) $y =$ _____ reaches its maximum point at the vertex. In both graphs the vertex coordinates are (24) (___,___)

Name ________________________ Date ________________________

Solving Quadratic Equations

The quadratic equation is in standard form when it is in the form $ax^2 + bx + c = y$. In solving equations, numbers will often replace the letters *a*, *b*, and *c* in the equation. For example: $2x^2 + 3x + 4 = y$; $-4x^2 + 8x + 1 = y$; and so forth.

Example: Solve $2x^2 + 3x + 4 = y$ if $x = 2$. The equation becomes $2 \cdot 2^2 + 3 \cdot 2 + 4 = y$, which becomes $8 + 6 + 4 = 18$.

Solve $-4x^2 + 8x + 1 = y$ if $x = 3$. The equation becomes $-4(3^2) + 8(3) + 1 = y$, which becomes $-36 + 24 + 1 = -11$.

Solve the following. The first one is completed.

1) $ax^2 + bx + c = y$ ($x = 2$, $a = 1$, $b = 3$, $c = 1$) a) $1 \cdot 2^2 + 3 \cdot 2 + 1 = y$

b) $4 + 6 + 1 = 10$ c) $10 = 10$

2) $2x^2 + 3x + 4 = y$ ($x = 1$) a) ____________ b) ________ c) ________

3) $-3x^2 + 4x + 4 = y$ ($x = 3$) a) ____________ b) ________ c) ________

4) $ax^2 + bx + c = y$ ($x = -3$, $a = -1$, $b = 3$, $c = 1$) a) ____________

b) ____________ c) ________

5) $ax^2 + bx + c = y$ ($x = 2$, $a = -4$, $b = 3$, $c = 1$) a) ____________

b) ____________ c) ________

6) $ax^2 + bx + c = y$ ($x = -2$, $a = -1$, $b = 3$, $c = 1$) a) ____________

b) ____________ c) ________

7) $2x^2 + 3x - 1 = y$ ($x = \frac{1}{2}$) a) ____________ b) ________ c) ________

8) $2x^2 + 3x - 2 = y$ ($x = -1$) a) ____________ b) ________ c) ________

9) $2x^2 + 3x + 6 = y$ ($x = \frac{1}{4}$) a) ____________ b) ________ c) ________

10) $2x^2 + 3x - 4 = y$ ($x = -4$) a) ____________ b) ________ c) ________

Name ______________________ Date ______________________

Standard Form of a Quadratic Equation

You have learned that the quadratic equation in **standard form** is $ax^2 + bx + c = y$. You have seen that when the equation is graphed the form is $y = ax^2 + bx + c$.

In many cases, however, the quadratic will not be in the **standard form**.

Example: $x^2 - 6x = -8$ is not in standard form. It is placed in standard form by adding +8 to each side of the equation. The equation is then written as $x^2 - 6x + 8 = -8 + 8$. The equation is then rewritten in standard form as $x^2 - 6x + 8 = 0$.

Rewrite each of the following in standard form. The first one has been completed.

1) $x^2 + 8x = -16$ a) $x^2 + 8x + 16 = -16 + 16$ b) $x^2 + 8x + 16 = 0$

2) $x^2 - 7x = -6$ a) ______ b) ______

3) $x^2 - 7x = -36$ a) ______ b) ______

4) $x^2 - 4x = -4$ a) ______ b) ______

5) $4x^2 - 16x = 20$ a) ______ b) ______

6) $10x^2 + 6x = 2$ a) ______ b) ______

7) $11x^2 + 3x = -4$ a) ______ b) ______

8) $5x^2 - 2x = -5$ a) ______ b) ______

9) $2x^2 + 2x = -2$ a) ______ b) ______

10) $7x^2 + x = 5$ a) ______ b) ______

Name ______________________________ Date ____________________________

Solving Quadratics by Factoring

There are several methods for solving quadratic equations. Two of the methods are (1) factoring and (2) using the quadratic formula.

Factoring: A quadratic is the product of two binomials. In factoring a quadratic you are finding the two binomials. x is a member of each binomial.

Example: Factor $x^2 - 4x + 4 = 0$

Step 1: Set up two binomials with x as the first member of each $(x - ?)(x - ?)$.

Step 2: Find two numbers that if added will equal $-4x$ and if multiplied will equal $+4$.

$$x^2 - 4x + 4 = (x - 2)(x - 2) = \begin{array}{r} x - 2 \\ \underline{x - 2} \\ x^2 - 2x \\ \underline{-2x + 4} \\ x^2 - 4x + 4 \end{array}$$

Once the equation is factored into $(x - 2)(x - 2)$, it is important to determine the number that must be substituted for "x" so that $(x - 2)(x - 2)$ equals zero. In this case if "x" equals +2 it will result in the problem 2 - 2, which is equal to zero. Therefore, $(x - 2)(x - 2)$ equals zero.

Each of the following quadratics can be solved by factoring. Find the factors and solve the equation. The first one has been completed. Remember **not all quadratics can be solved by factoring.**

1) $x^2 + 4x - 12 = 0$ a) $(x + 6)(x - 2)$ b) $x = -6$ or $x = 2$

2) $x^2 - 6x + 9 = 0$ a) ____________ b) ____________

3) $x^2 + 5x + 6 = 0$ a) ____________ b) ____________

4) $x^2 - 10x + 24 = 0$ a) ____________ b) ____________

5) $x^2 - 7x + 12 = 0$ a) ____________ b) ____________

6) $x^2 + 8x + 16 = 0$ a) ____________ b) ____________

7) $x^2 - 2x + 1 = 0$ a) ____________ b) ____________

8) $x^2 - 7x + 10 = 0$ a) ____________ b) ____________

9) $x^2 + 3x + 2 = 0$ a) ____________ b) ____________

10) $y^2 + 2y - 3 = 0$ a) ____________ b) ____________

Name ______________________________ Date ______________________________

Solving Quadratics by the Quadratic Formula

The solution to any quadratic equation can be found using the quadratic formula. You will study the development of the quadratic formula and why it works in your study of algebra. The purpose of this exercise is to introduce the quadratic formula and provide some exercises in how it can be used.

The quadratic formula is $x = \dfrac{-b \pm \sqrt{b^2 - 4ac}}{2a}$

Example: Solve $x^2 - 4x - 5 = 0$ using the formula.
In using the formula, it is important to think of the quadratic equation in standard form $ax^2 + bx + c = 0$. $x^2 - 4x - 5 = 0$ is in standard form.
When the equation $x^2 - 4x - 5 = 0$ is in standard form, $a = 1$, $b = -4$, and $c = -5$.
Now to solve the equation $x^2 - 4x - 5 = 0$ using the formula, the numbers for a, b, and c must be substituted in the equation.

The quadratic formula $x = \dfrac{-b \pm \sqrt{b^2 - 4ac}}{2a}$ becomes $x = \dfrac{-(-4) \pm \sqrt{(-4)^2 - 4(1)(-5)}}{2(1)}$

becomes $x = \dfrac{-(-4) \pm \sqrt{16 + 20}}{2}$ becomes $x = \dfrac{4 \pm \sqrt{36}}{2}$ becomes $x = \dfrac{4 \pm 6}{2}$

becomes $x = 5$ or $x = -1$.

Now $x = 5$ or $x = -1$. To determine if $x = 5$ or $x = -1$ is the correct solution to the quadratic, each must be substituted into the equation $x^2 - 4x - 5 = 0$.

$x = -1$ $(-1)^2 - 4(-1) - 5 = 0$ -1 is a solution
$x = 5$ $5^2 - 4(5) - 5 = 0$ +5 is a solution

Solve the following. Substitute the numbers for a, b, and c in the formula, and determine the possible solutions for x. Then substitute each possible solution into the equation, and determine the solution. Show all the steps you take in solving the equation. The first one has been completed.

1) $x^2 + 6x - 16 = 0$ $a = 1$, $b = 6$, $c = -16$

$x = \dfrac{-b \pm \sqrt{b^2 - 4ac}}{2a} = \dfrac{-(+6) \pm \sqrt{(6)^2 - 4(1)(-16)}}{2(1)} = \dfrac{-6 \pm \sqrt{36 + 64}}{2(1)} = \dfrac{-6 \pm \sqrt{100}}{2(1)} =$

$\dfrac{-6 + 10}{2} = \dfrac{+4}{2} = +2$ or $\dfrac{-6 - 10}{2} = \dfrac{-16}{2} = -8$

Possible solutions to the equation
+2 and -8

Check: $x^2 + 6x - 16 = 0 = (2)^2 + 6(2) - 16 = 0$
Check: $x^2 + 6x - 16 = 0 = (-8)^2 + 6(-8) - 16 = 0$ Solution: +2, -8

Name ______________________________ Date ____________________________

Solving Quadratics by the Quadratic Formula (continued)

2) $x^2 - 2x - 8 = 0$ $a = 1$ $b = -2$ $c = -8$

Possible solutions to equation: _______ _______

Check: ____

Solution: ___________

3) $x^2 - 2x - 4 = 0$ $a = 1$ $b = -2$ $c = -4$

Possible solutions to equation: _______ _______

Check: ____

Solution: ___________

4) $x^2 + 2x - 1 = 0$ $a = 1$ $b = 2$ $c = -1$

Possible solutions to equation: _______ _______

Check: ____

Solution: ___________

5) $2x^2 + x - 5 = 0$ $a = 2$ $b = 1$ $c = -5$

Possible solutions to equation: _______ _______

Check: ____

Solution: ___________

Name ______________________________ Date ______________________________

Quiz X: Learning About Quadratic Equations

Fill in the blanks with the correct word. Select answers from the following list.

factoring	**quadratic equation**	**formula**	**second degree**	**c**
numbers	**completing the square**	**standard form**	**numbers**	

The equation $x^2 + 2x + 4$ is a (1) ____________ ____________. It is a quadratic equation because it is a (2)__________ __________ polynomial equation. Quadratic equations may be solved by (3) ____________ and by using the quadratic (4) ________.

When the quadratic is written as $ax^2 + bx + c = y$, it is in the (5) ____________ ____________. In $ax^2 + bx + c = y$ the letters a, b, and c will be replaced by (6) ________. In the quadratic equation, the letter (7)___ remains constant no matter what value is given to x.

Rewrite each of the following in standard form.

8) $5x^2 - 2x = 6$ ______________________________

9) $8x^2 + 6x = -4$ ______________________________

Solve the following by factoring.

10) $6x^2 + 4x - 10 = y$ ______________________________

11) $3x^2 + 19x + 20 = y$ ______________________________

12) $4x^2 + 5x - 6 = y$ ______________________________

Solve the following using the quadratic formula.

13) $2x^2 + 3x - 2 = 0$

14) $x^2 + 4x + 3 = 0$

Solution: ____________

Solution: ____________

Answer Keys

Understanding the Real Number System (page 1)

1) 5–14
2) 51, 52, 53…58–63
3) 1,235–1,238…1,240, 1,241
4) 7–18
5) 24–29…32, 33, 34…36
6) 225–231
7) -12–(-5)…5–16
8) -10,008–(-10,001)

Real Numbers (page 2)

1) Does not work.
2) Does not work.
3) 0.0000…

fractions are numbers:
4, 5, 6, 9, 10

Quotient Questions (page 3)

1) 0.6
2) 0.875
3) 0.88888888…
4) 1 ÷ 6; 0.166666666…
5) 4 ÷ 5; 0.8
6) 0.58333333…
7) 0.428571429…
8) 0.5625
9) 0.03125
10) 0.81818181…
11) 0.866666666…
12) 5
13) 7
14) 56
15) 9
16) 88
17) (any order) a) $\frac{1}{32}$ b) $\frac{9}{1}$ c) $\frac{56}{1}$ d) $\frac{7}{1}$ e) $\frac{88}{1}$ f) $\frac{4}{5}$ g) $\frac{9}{16}$ h) $\frac{5}{1}$
18) (any order) a) $\frac{3}{7}$ b) $\frac{9}{11}$ c) $\frac{7}{12}$ d) $\frac{1}{6}$ e) $\frac{13}{15}$
19) repeating, non-repeating
20) denominator

Rational Numbers (page 4)

1) $-\frac{2}{1}$
2) $-1\frac{3}{4}$
3) $-1\frac{1}{2}$
4) $-1\frac{3}{8}$
5) $-\frac{1}{1}$
6) $-\frac{3}{4}$
7) $-\frac{1}{8}$
8) $+\frac{1}{8}$
9) $+\frac{3}{4}$
10) $+\frac{1}{1}$
11) $+1\frac{3}{8}$
12) $+1\frac{1}{2}$
13) $+1\frac{3}{4}$
14) $+\frac{2}{1}$

Irrational Numbers (page 6)

1) a) 2 b) rational
2) a) 3 b) rational
3) a) 2.645751311… b) irrational
4) a) 3.31662479… b) irrational
5) a) 3.464101615… b) irrational
6) a) 4.242640687… b) irrational
7) a) 4.123105626… b) irrational
8) a) 12 b) rational
9) a) 12.489996 b) irrational
10) a) 11.18033989… b) irrational
11) a) 6 b) rational
12) a) 6.92820323… b) irrational
13) a) 7 b) rational
14) a) 5.099019514… b) irrational

Chart:

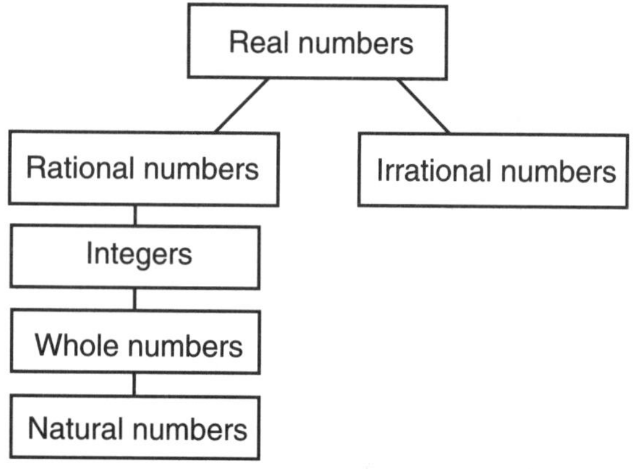

Quiz I: Number Systems (page 7)
1) 0
2) integers
3) rational
4)irrational
5) B
6) A
7) C
8) E
9) D
10) rational
11) irrational
12) rational
13) rational
14) rational
15) rational
16) rational
17) irrational
18) rational
19) rational
20) irrational

Adding Positive and Negative Numbers (page 8)
1) +6, A
2) -15, A
3) -2, B
4) +2, B
5) +4, B
6) -11, A
7) +24, A
8) +13, B
9) -68, A
10) +2, B
11) +101, B
12) +11, B
13) +156, A
14) +3
15) -22
16) +9
17) -143
18) +376
19) +86
20) -11
21) -22
22) -67
23) -129
24) -101
25) -39

Subtracting Positive and Negative Numbers (page 9)
1) +5, +14
2) -14, -26
3) +18, -107
4) +23, +38
5) +13
6) -35
7) -9
8) difference

Quiz II: Addition and Subtraction with Positive and Negative Numbers (page 10)
1) 90 (addend)
+ -123 (addend)
-33 (sum)
2) +79
3) -55
4) +89
5) +99
6) +89
7) +135
8) -523
9) 90 (minuend)
- -123 (subtrahend)
213 (difference)
10) +11
11) -73
12) +159
13) +99
14) -467
15) +343
16) -455
17) C
18) E
19) D
20) B
21) A

Multiplication with Positive and Negative Numbers (page 11)

1) +32; for like signs, multiply and place a positive sign in front of the product
2) -480; for unlike signs, multiply and place the negative sign in front of the product
3) -35; for unlike signs, multiply and place the negative sign in front of the product
4) +405; for like signs, multiply and place a positive sign in front of the product
5) -60; for unlike signs, multiply and place the negative sign in front of the product
6) +364; for like signs, multiply and place a positive sign in front of the product
7) +312; for like signs, multiply and place a positive sign in front of the product
8) -536; for unlike signs, multiply and place the negative sign in front of the product

More Multiplication with Positive and Negative Numbers (page 12)

1) 84
2) 360
3) -560
4) -56
5) 288
6) -612
7) 390
8) 504
9) 840
10) 1,080
11) 4,320
12) 60,480

Division with Positive and Negative Numbers (page 13)

1) 6; For like signs, find the quotient and place the positive sign in front of quotient.
2) -6; For unlike signs, find the quotient and place the negative sign in front of the quotient.
3) 6; For like signs, find the quotient and place the positive sign in front of quotient.
4) -6; For unlike signs, find the quotient and place the negative sign in front of the quotient.
5) 128
6) 25
7) -26
8) 56

Quiz III: Multiplication and Division with Positive and Negative Numbers (page 14)

1) -322
2) 117
3) -5,412
4) 180,900
5) -18,564
6) -246
7) 98,496
8) -25,920
9) 10
10) -108
11) 1,800
12) -17,820
13) 181,440
14) -6,048
15) 19,800
16) will have *positive* sign
17) will have *negative* sign
18) -6
19) 4
20) 8
21) -25
22) 76
23) -48
24) will have the sign of the *negative* number
25)will have *a positive* sign

Equal, Less Than, Greater Than (page 16)

1) <
2) >
3) <
4) >
5) <
6) <
7) >
8) >
9) <
10) >
11) =
12) =

13) <
14) =
15) <
16) <
17) <
18) >
19) >
20) <
21) <
22) =
23) >
24) =
25) <

More Mathematical Symbols (pages 17–18)

1) -12
2) 29
3) 11
4) 48
5) 4
6) 12
7) 105
8) 13

All (numbers 1–8) are constants because all letters represent only one possible number value.

9–16) Answers will vary depending on the number chosen as the numerical value for each.

17) 8–20
18) 84–96
19) 1–6
20) 2–6

All (numbers 9–20) are variables because all letters have several possible numeric values.

Problems With More Than One Variable (page 19)

1) (0,6); (-1,7); (-2, 8); (5, 1); (4, 2); (3,3); and vise versa
2) none
3) none
4) (5, 5); (-5, -5)
5) (5, 5); (-5, -5)
6) (2, -1); (1, -2); (0, -3); (3, 0); (4, 1); (5, 2); (6, 3); (7, 4); (8,5)
7) 20
8) 28
9) -28
10) 14
11) 17
12) -7
13) 6
14) -3
15) -8
16) 11
17) -28
18) -21
19) -2
20) 0

Word Problems Using Variables (page 20)

1) a
2) b
3) $4.50; $10.00
4) a) $4.50; $10.00
b) $4.50; $14.50
c) $4.50; $12.50
d) $4.50; $8.00

Letter "d" is the correct answer.

5) 2x - 1 = $8.00
6) 2; 4.50; 1.00
7) teacher check

Quiz IV: Mathematical Symbols (page 21)

1) H
2) J
3) B
4) D
5) A
6) C
7) L
8) F
9) K
10) G
11) E
12) I
13–18) teacher check

Understanding Polynomials (page 22)
The following numbers should have plus signs in front of them:
2, 3, 5, 6, 7, 8, 10, 12, 14, 15, 16, 19, 20, 23, 26, 28, 29, 30, 34, 36, 39, 40

Terms, Expressions, and Polynomials (page 23)
The following should have plus signs in front of them:
1, 2, 3, 6, 9, 11, 13, 14, 15, 16, 18, 19, 23
24) M
25) B
26) B
27) T
28) T
29) M
30) M
31) B
32) M
33) T
34) B
35) M

Adding Polynomials (page 25)
1) $2x^2$; x^2
2)$7x^3$; x^3
3) y^4; $3y^4$
4) p^4; $2p^4$
5) t^4; $3t^4$; $10t^4$
6) $4x$; $2x$
7) $8y^3$; $5y^3$; y^3 and x^3; $2x^3$
8) k; $3k$; $6k$
9) none
10) $10x^2$; $2x^2$; x^2
11) x
12) $6y$
13) $3x$
14) $7x$
15) $4x^2 - 3x + 2y^2$
16) $2x^2 - 3y^2$
17) $3y^2 - 4x^2$
18) $2x^4 - x^3 + x^2 + 2y$
19) $2x^4 - x^3 + x^2 + 2y$
20) $-5x^4 - x^3 + x^2 + y^3$

Subtracting Polynomials (page 26)
1) $xy - 4x + 4y + 27$
2) $-5x + b$
3) $x^3 - 3x^2 - 2x + 2y$
4) $x + 4y - 3a$
5) $12x^3 - x + 11y^2 + 2y$
6) $11x^3 + 11y^2 + 2y$
7) $-13x^3 - 9y^2$
8) $-11x^3 - 11y^2 - 2y$

Multiplying Polynomials (pages 27–28)
1) $3x - 3y$
2) $3x^2 + 3xy$
3) $t^6 - t^2y^2$
4) $-2x^3 - 2x^2 + 2xy$
5) $9xy^3$
6) $-15x^4 + 10x^3 - 5x^2y + 5xy$
7) $15x^4 - 10x^3 + 5x^2y - 5xy$
8) $-42x^2y^3$
9) $42x^3y^3$
10) $-3a^5$
11) $3x^2 + xy - 2y^2$
12) $x^3 + x - x^2y - y$
13) $-3x^4 + x^2y^3 + 3x^2y^2 - y^5$
14) $-x^2 + y^2$
15) $x^2 + xy^3 - y^4 - xy$
16) $2t^2 - 3x^4t + x^8$

Dividing Polynomials (pages 29–30)
1) x^2
2) y^4
3) t
4) $2x^2$
5) $4y$
6) x^2
7) x^{-2} or $\frac{1}{x^2}$
8) y^{-4} or $\frac{1}{y^4}$
9) t^{-1} or $\frac{1}{t}$
10) $-2x^2$
11) $-4y$
12) x^2
13) $7x^3 + 3x^2$
14) $y - 1$
15) $3r^3 - 4r + 2r^{-1}$or $3r^3 - 4r + \frac{2}{r}$
16) $-7x^3 + -3x^2$

17) $-y - (-x/y)$ or $-y + \frac{x}{y}$
18) $-7x^3 + 3x^2$
19) $b + s$
20) $2c - a$

Quiz V: Understanding Polynomials (pages 31–32)

1) D
2) F
3) A
4) C
5) B
6) E
7) H
8) G
9) I
10) J
11) x^2; $5x^2$
12) $y^2 + 15y$
13) $8x^2 + 7x - 11y$
14) $8y^2 - 7y$
15) $17x^3 + 3y^3 - 6y^2 + 5$
16) $6x^5 + 3x^3y - 4x^2y - 2y^2$
17) $x^6 + x^5 - 2x^4$
18) $3y^2$
19) $-3y^{-2}$ or $-3/y^2$
20) $4y^3 - 2y^2 - y$

Written and Mathematical Expressions (pages 33–34)

1) $7 + y$ or $y + 7$
2) $y - 3$
3) $10 + y$ or $y + 10$
4) $y - 13$
5) $y - 7$
6) $8y$
7) $5y + 3$
8) $9y$
9) $3y + 5$
10) $2y - 16$
11) $y + 40$ or $40 + y$
12) $y + \frac{1}{5}$
13) $y - \frac{2}{3}$
14) $(y/10) - 6$
15) $(y/8) + 5$
16) $5y + 6 = 50$
17) $(y/5) - 7 = 37$
18) $y + 17 + 3 - 12 = 15$
19) $y - 8 = 12$
20) $13y = 117$
21) $5y = 55$
22) $5y + 6 = 2y + 45$
23) $3y = y + 15$
24) $2y + 17 = 48$
25) $2y + 7 = 23$
26) $\frac{1}{3} + 7y = 100$
27) $7y + 13 = 127 + y$
28) $1{,}000 \div 3 = y$
29) $2(1\frac{1}{2}) = y$
30) $30 = 2y - 1$
31) $P = 2W + 2L$
32) $a = LW$
33) $\frac{1}{2}bh = a$ or $bh/2 = a$
34) $a = \pi r^2$
35) $C = (F - 32)\frac{5}{9}$

Equations (page 35)

1) 4
2) 1
3) 5, 8
4) 10, 3
5) 6
6) 6
7) 21, 3
8) 7
9) 4, 8
10) 5

Review of Equation Rules (pages 38–39)

Final answers (part b):

1) 21
2) 12
3) 70
4) 28
5) 7
6) 14
7) 40
8) 10
9) 16
10) 27

11) 64
12) 3,125
13) 60
(part c):
14) 5
15) 64
16) 1
17) 100
18) 14

Learning About Parentheses and Brackets (pages 40–41)
Final answer (part d):
1) 6
2) 1
3) 2
4) 3
5) 5
6) -8
7) 3
8) 2

Order of Operations (pages 42–43)
Final answer
1) 3
2) 2
3) 29
4) -10
5) 9
6) -7
7) 10
8) 6
9) -253
10) 8
11) $5x - 5y - z = x$
12) $8x = 14a$
13) $-\frac{3}{2} = x$
14) $\frac{1}{3} = x$
15) $3z - 4a - 4b + x/y = x$
16) $-4.8 = x$

Quiz VI: Learning About Equations (page 44)
1) mathematical statement
2) equality
3) $2x + 1 = 7$
4) algebraic expressions
5) equal
6) equality
7) added
8) subtracted
9) zero
10) divided
11) left, right
12) parentheses
13) negative
14) positive
15) left, right
16) multiplication, division
17) addition, subtraction
18) simplified
19) $x = -1/6$
20) $2y - 8 = -x$
21) C
22) A
23) B
24) E
25) D

Understanding and Using Exponents (page 45)
1) 64
2) 27
3) 49
4) 100,000
5) 2,744
6) 16,777,216
7) 19,487,171
8) 40,353,607
9) 46,656
10) 248,832

Exponents, Bases, and Factors (page 46)
1) 4
2) 8
3) 16
4) 64
5) 9
6) 27

7) 81
8) 243
9) 16
10) 64
11) 256
12) 1,024
13) 100
14) 1,000
15) 10,000
16) 100,000

Exponents in Algebraic Expressions (page 47)

1) 4
2) 27
3) 3,125
4) 28
5) 255
6) 8
7) 12
8) 60
9) 16
10) 48
11) 108
12) 130
13) 54
14) 52
15) 499
16) $9\frac{1}{25}$

Looking for Patterns When Using Exponents (page 48)

1) 3
2) 9
3) 27
4) 81
5) c
6) c
7) c
8) 3
9) $\frac{81}{243}$
10) $\frac{27}{81}$
11) $\frac{9}{27}$
12) $\frac{3}{9}$
13) $\frac{1}{3}$
14) $\frac{1}{3}$
15) $\frac{1}{3}$
16) $\frac{1}{3}$
17) 1
18) all equal 1
19) a) 32; b) 16; c) 8; d) 4; e) 2; f) 1
20) b

Expressing Exponents in Words (page 49)

1) Three to the second power.
2) Five to the third power.
3) Four to the fourth power.
4) Ten to the third power.
5) Seven to the fifth power.
6) Fourty-two to the first power.
7) a) 8^2 b) 64
8) a) 12^8 b) 429,981,696
9) a) 2^6 b) 64
10) a) 4^0 b) 1
11) a) 6^2 b) 36
12) a) 3^4 b) 81
13) a) 7^1 b) 7
14) a) 5^3 b) 125
15) a) 25^5 b) 9,765,625

Dealing With Negative Exponents and Negative Bases (page 50)

Final answer:
1) $\frac{1}{4}$
2) $\frac{1}{81}$
3) $\frac{1}{64}$
4) $\frac{1}{216}$
5) $\frac{1}{125}$
6) $\frac{1}{100}$
7) 9
8) -243
9) 27
10) -64
11) 125
12) -512
13) -512
14) 25
15) 16

Adding, Subtracting, and Multiplying Exponents (pages 51–52)

1) a) 5^{2+1}; b) 5^3; c) 125
2) a) 6^{3+2}; b) 6^5; c) 7,776
3) a) 7^{3+5}; b) 7^8; c) 5,764,801
4) a) x^{3+2}; b) x^5
5) a) y^{1+4}; b) y^5
6) a) r^{4+2}; b) r^6
7) a) $2^{2 \cdot 3}$; b) 2^6; c) 64
8) a) $2^{4 \cdot 2}$; b) 2^8; c) 256
9) a) $10^{3 \cdot 2}$; b) 10^6; c) 1,000,000
10) a) $7^{1 \cdot 5}$; b) 7^5; c) 16,807
11) a) $5^{3 \cdot 3}$; b) 5^9; c) 1,953,125
12) a) $12^{2 \cdot 2}$; b) 12^4; c) 20,736
13) a) $3^{3 \cdot 4}$; b) 3^{12}; c) 531,441
14) a) $2^{5 \cdot 2}$; b) 2^{10}; c) 1,024
15) a) $3^{2 \cdot 2}$; b) 3^4; c) 81
16) a) $6^{1 \cdot 3}$; b) 6^3; c) 216
17) a) 6^{4-2}; b) 6^2; c) 36
18) a) 7^{5-4}; b) 7^1; c) 7
19) a) 2^{6-3}; b) 2^3; c) 8
20) a) 4^{2-5}; b) 4^{-3}; c) $1/4^3$; d) $\frac{1}{64}$
21) a) 3^{1-6}; b) 3^{-5}; c) $1/3^5$; d) $\frac{1}{243}$
22) a) x^{4-2}; b) x^2
23) a) y^{6-3}; b) y^3
24) a) x^{4-6}; b) x^{-2}; c) $1/x^2$
25) a) y^{7-8}; b) y^{-1}; c) $1/y$

Quiz VII: Understanding and Using Exponents (page 53)

1) Four to the sixth power.
2) Three to the fifth power.
3) Two to the fourth power.
4) a) 3; b) 5, 5, 5
5) a) 5; b) 10, 10, 10, 10, 10
6) a) 6; b) 3, 3, 3, 3, 3, 3
7) a) 4; b) *y, y, y, y*
8) 125
9) 1
10) 10,000
11) 64
12) 64
13) 16
14) 1
15) 125
16) 12
17) 270
18) 96
19) $\frac{1}{4}$
20) $\frac{1}{3}$
21) $\frac{1}{25}$
22) 625; 125; 25; 5; 1; $\frac{1}{5}$; $\frac{1}{25}$; $\frac{1}{125}$; $\frac{1}{625}$
23) b
24) a) $\frac{1}{5}$; b) $\frac{1}{5}$
25) 4,782,969
26) 161,051
27) 390,625
28) 117,649
29) 4,096
30) $\frac{1}{4096}$

Learning How to Read and Write Radicals (page 55)

1–10) teacher check
11) $\sqrt{64}$
12) $\sqrt[3]{125}$
13) $\sqrt[4]{64}$
14) $\sqrt[8]{256}$
15) $\sqrt[5]{1{,}024}$
16) $\sqrt{3}$
17) $\sqrt{2}$
18) $\sqrt[3]{27}$
19) $\sqrt[4]{81}$
20) $\sqrt[3]{1{,}000}$

Number of Factors (page 56)

1) a) 3; b) 3 • 3 • 3 • 3
2) a) 5; b) 5 • 5 • 5
3) a) 4; b) 4 • 4 • 4 • 4
4) a) 4; b) 4 • 4 • 4 • 4 • 4
5) a) 3; b) 3 • 3
6) a) 1.414213562…; b) irrational; c) 2
7) a) 1.732050808…; b) irrational; c) 2
8) a) 1.903653939…; b) irrational; c) 5
9) a) 2; b) rational; c) 3
10) a) 6.164414003…; b) irrational; c) 2

Adding Radicals (page 57)

Final answer:

1) $7\sqrt{9}$
2) $3\sqrt{5}$
3) $6\sqrt{13}$
4) $15\sqrt{156}$
5) $6\sqrt{7}$
6) $8\sqrt{8}$
7) $8\sqrt{5}$
8) $2\sqrt{2}$
9) $5\sqrt{2}$
10) $2\sqrt{2}$
11) $10\sqrt{7}$
12) $6\sqrt{2}$

Subtracting Radicals (page 58)

Final answer:

1) $3\sqrt{2}$
2) $1\sqrt{7}$
3) $5\sqrt{3}$
4) $8\sqrt{8}$
5) 0 or $0\sqrt{12}$
6) $1\sqrt{4}$
7) $1\sqrt{10}$
8) $3\sqrt{2}$
9) $-3\sqrt{16}$
10) $3\sqrt{9}$ or 9
11) $7\sqrt{10}$
12) $2\sqrt{3}$
13) $4\sqrt{3}$
14) $4\sqrt{6}$
15) $2\sqrt{20}$

Multiplying Radicals (page 59)

1) a) $\sqrt{16}$; b) 4; c) rational
2) a) $\sqrt{12}$; b) 3.464101615…; c) irrational
3) a) $\sqrt{16}$; b) 4; c) rational
4) a) $9\sqrt{125}$; b) 100.623059…; c) irrational
5) a) $4\sqrt{64}$; b) 32; c) rational
6) a) $25\sqrt{xy}$
7) a) $8\sqrt{xyz}$
8) a) $64\sqrt{48}$; b) 443.4050067…; c) irrational
9) a) $5\sqrt[4]{81}$; b) 15; c) rational
10) a) $8\sqrt[3]{16}$; b) 20.1587368…; c) irrational

Dividing Radicals (page 60)

1) a) $\frac{18}{2}$; b) $\sqrt{9}$; c) 3; d) rational
2) a) $\frac{8}{2}$; b) $\sqrt{4}$; c) 2; d) rational
3) a) $\frac{48}{2}$; b) $\sqrt{24}$; c) 4.898979486…; d) irrational
4) a) $\frac{16}{4}$; b) $\sqrt{4}$; c) 2; d) rational
5) a) $\frac{125}{5}$; b) $\sqrt{25}$; c) 5; d) rational
6) a) $\frac{125}{5}$; b) $\sqrt[3]{25}$; c) 2.924017738…; d) irrational
7) a) $\frac{64}{2}$; b) $\sqrt[5]{32}$; c) 2; d) rational
8) a) x/y; b) $\sqrt[4]{x/y}$
9) a) x/y; b) $\sqrt{x/y}$
10) a) x/y; b) $\sqrt[3]{x/y}$

Prime Factors and Simplifying Square Root Radicals (page 61–62)

1) 2, 7
2) 2, 3, 2, 2, 2
3) 2, 3, 5, 2, 5, 2
4) 2, 2, 2, 2, 2, 2, 2, 2, 2
5) 2, 7, 17
6) 2, 2, 2, 2, 2, 3
7) 5, 5, 5, 2, 2
8) a) 2, 2, 3; b) 3.464101615…
9) a) 3, 3, 7; b) 7.937253933…
10) a) 2, 2, 3; b) 6.92820323…
11) a) 2, 3, 3, 3; b) 7.348469228…
12) a) 2, 2, 3; b) $2\sqrt{3}$; c) 3, 3, 2; d) $3\sqrt{2}$; e) $2\sqrt{3} + 3\sqrt{2} = 7.706742302…$

Rationalizing the Denominators in Radicals With Fractions (page 63)

1) $\frac{2\sqrt{5}}{5}$
2) $\frac{\sqrt{6}}{3}$
3) $\frac{\sqrt{2}}{2}$
4) 5
5) 2

Learning About Radicals in Equations (page 64)

Final answers:
1) $x = 9$
2) $x = 16$
3) $x = 81$
4) $x = 25$
5) $x = 36$
6) $x = 49$
7) $x = 64$
8) $x = 144$
9) $x = 225$
10) $x = 100$

Quiz VIII: Learning About Radicals and Roots (page 65)

1) $\sqrt{49}$
2) $\sqrt[4]{64}$
3) $\sqrt[3]{125}$
4) $\sqrt[8]{256}$
5) square root of eight
6) cubed root of eight
7) sixth root of seventy-eight
8) a) 9; b) 9 • 9
9) a) 2; b) 2 • 2 • 2 • 2
10) a) 3; b) 3 • 3 • 3
11) a) 2; b) 2 • 2 • 2 • 2 • 2
12) $\sqrt{14}$
13) $\sqrt{35}$
14) $2\sqrt{18}$
15) $\sqrt{3}$
16) $\sqrt{3}$
17) $\sqrt{7}$
18) $2\sqrt{3}$
19) $15\sqrt{2}$
20) $\frac{\sqrt{3}}{2}$
21) $\frac{\sqrt{6}}{3}$
22) indexes, radicands
23) because both are square roots and both have radicands of twelve
24) indexes, radicands
25) both are square roots, but the radicands are different

Learning About Linear Equations (page 66)

First degree equations are: 2, 3, 5, 6, 7

Determining the Slope of a Graphed Linear Equation (pages 67–69)

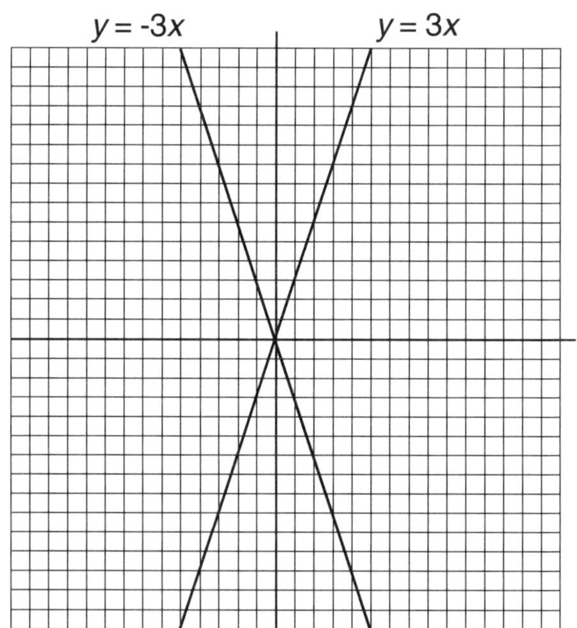

1) straight
2) first
3) linear
4) x; y; 0; 0
5) up; right; positive
6) up; left; positive
7) down; left; negative

8) $y = 3x$; When read left to right it slopes upward.
9) $y = -3x$; When read left to right it slopes downward.

Positive and Negative Slope (page 70)
1) b
2) up
3) positive
4) a
5) c
6) a
7) c
8) a
9) a
10) c
11) a
12) b

Formula for Determining the Slope of a Graphed Linear Equation (page 71)
1) Letters a, c, d, e, and f should be marked.
2) teacher check

Graphing Linear Equations and Determining Their Slopes (pages 72–73)
1–3) teacher check

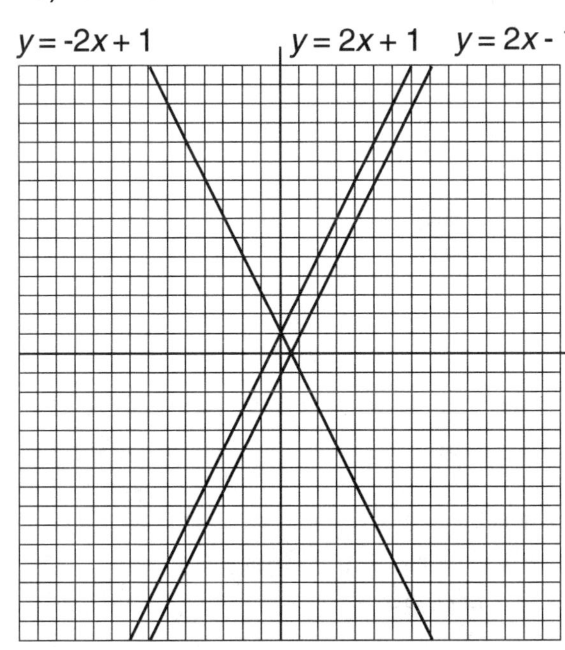

4) positive
5–6) teacher check
7) 2
8) positive
9–10) teacher check
11) 2
12) negative
13–14) teacher check
15) -2

Learning About the *x*-Intercept and *y*-Intercept (pages 74–75)

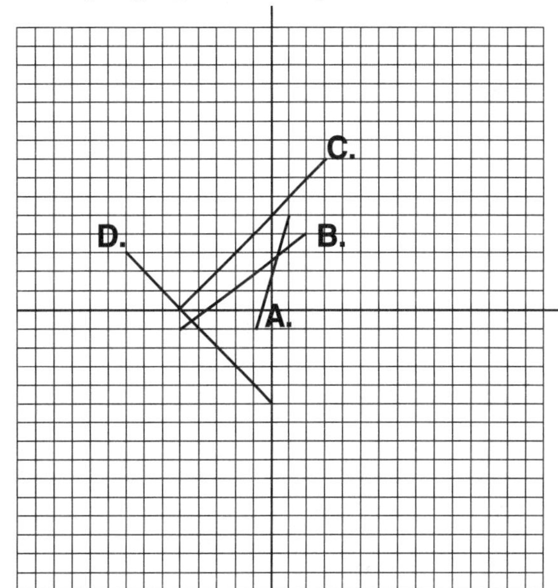

1) A, B, C
2) D
3) 0,2
4) 0,2
5) $-\frac{2}{3}$,0
6) $-\frac{2}{3}$,0
7) $\frac{2}{3}$,0
8) 0,-2
9) -5,0
10) 0,5
11) -5,0
12) 0,-5
13) c
14) c
15) 0; -4
16) x; 1
17) 0; 2
18) x; -2
19) 0
20) 0

Learning About the Slope Intercept Equation (pages 76–77)

1–4) teacher check
5) c
6) a
7) a
8–11) teacher check
12) a
13) c
14) c
15–18) teacher check
19) d
20) b
21) d
22) $\frac{3}{1}$; 3
23) 3
24) -8

Slope Intercept Exercises (page 78)

1) $y = 2x + 1$
2) $y = 2x + 8$
3) $y = x + 7$
4) $y = (x + 2)/3$
5) a) $\frac{4}{1}$; b) 5
6) a) $\frac{1}{2}$; b) -2
7) a) $\frac{1}{1}$; b) 1
8) a) $\frac{1}{1}$; b) 1
9) true
10) true
11) false
12) false
13) d
14) positive

Graphing Linear Equations (page 79)

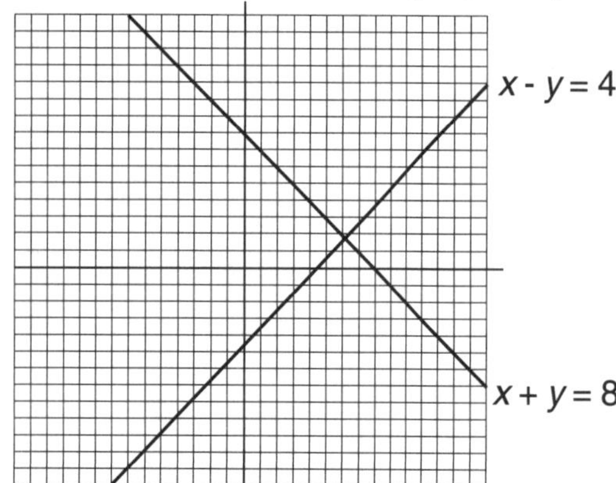

1) b
2a) $6 + 2 = 8$ b) $6 - 2 = 4$
3a) 6,2 b) $x + y = 8$ c) $x - y = 4$

Reviewing What You Have Learned (page 80)

Polynomials: 1, 2, 4, 5, 8, 9, 10, 11, 14, 15
Monomials: 3, 6, 7, 12, 13
Binomials: 1, 9, 10, 14
Trinomials: 2, 4, 5, 8, 11, 15
Linear: 1, 2, 10, 14
First degree: 1, 2, 8, 10, 13, 14
Algebraic: 4, 5, 6, 7, 9, 11, 12, 15

Quiz IX: Learning About Linear Equations (page 81)

1) linear equation
2) one
3) positive
4) negative
5) up
6) down
7) $y = -2x + 4$
8) negative
9) $y = 2x + 4$
10) positive
11) $y = mx + b$
12) m
13) b
14) vertical
15) horizontal
16) numerator
17) denominator
18) 10
19) 2

Learning About Quadratic Equations (page 82)

1) $x^5 + x^3 + x^2 - y$
2) $a^4 + a^3 - a^2$
3) $-4y^4 + 5xy^3 + y^2 - 2$
4) $b^4 - b^3 + 5b^2 + 10b$
5) $x^2 + x - y$
6) $-t^4 + t^3x^2 + 7t^2y^5 + a^3t$
7) $4y^5q^8 + q^3x^2 + 9q$
8) $d^9g^4 + 6d^2r - 2d$

9) $r^8x + 3r^5t - 2a^4r^2 - 4ar$
10) $-8y^3b^2 + y^2x^4 + 6yt^2 + 2y$

Graphing the Equation $ax^2 + bx + c$ (pages 83–84)

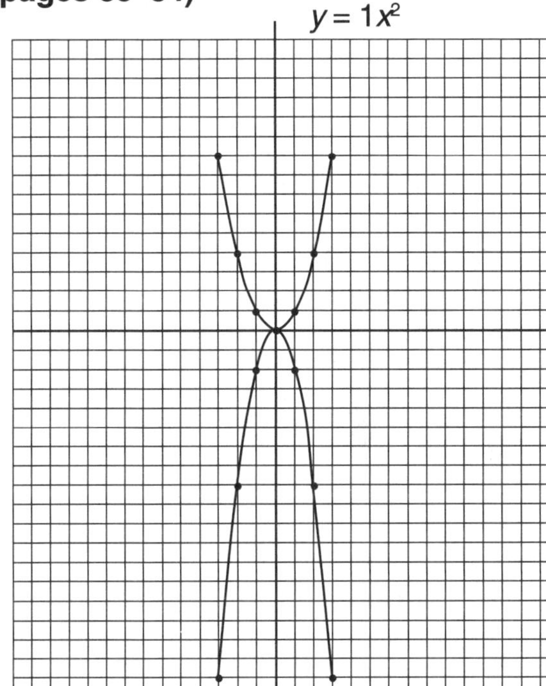

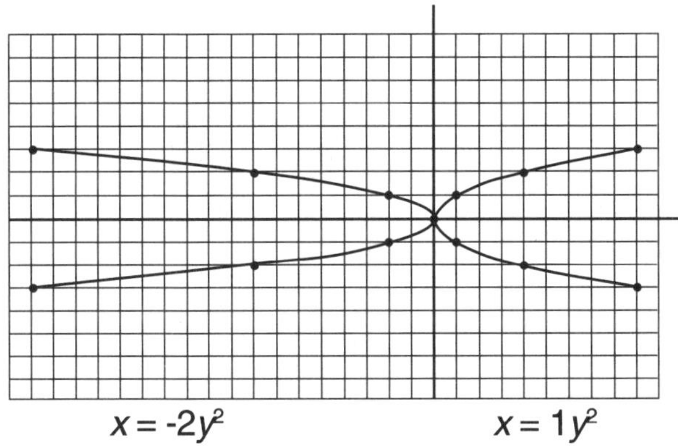

Parabolas (pages 85–86)
1) 1,0
2) decreasing
3) -1,0
4) increasing
5) 1,0
6) decreasing
7) 1,0
8) decreasing
9) maximum
10) minimum
11) vertex
12) -1,0
13) increasing
14) -1,0
15) increasing
16) -1,0
17) increasing
18) 1,0
19) decreasing
20) maximum
21) minimum
22) vertex

Parabola Practice (page 87)
1) a
2) teacher check
3) a
4) a
5) teacher check
6) c
7) b
8) a
9) teacher check
10) a
11) a
12) teacher check
13) d
14) d
15) teacher check
16) teacher check
17) true
18) *y*
19) two halves that are mirror images
20) symmectric
21) parabola
22) $y = ax^2$
23) $y = -2x^2$
24) 0,0

Solving Quadratic Equations (page 88)
Final answers are:
1) 10
2) 9
3) -11
4) -17
5) -9
6) -9
7) 1
8) -3
9) 55/8
10) 16

Standard Form of a Quadratic Equation (page 89)
Final answers are:
1) $x^2 + 8x + 16 = 0$
2) $x^2 - 7x + 6 = 0$
3) $x^2 - 7x + 36 = 0$
4) $x^2 - 4x + 4 = 0$
5) $4x^2 - 16x - 20 = 0$
6) $10x^2 + 6x -2 = 0$
7) $11x^2 + 3x + 4 = 0$
8) $5x^2 -2x + 5 = 0$
9) $2x^2 + 2x + 2 = 0$
10) $7x^2 + x - 5 = 0$

Solving Quadratics by Factoring (page 90)
1) a) $(x + 6)(x - 2)$; b) $x = -6$ or $x = 2$
2) a) $(x - 3)(x - 3)$; b) $x = 3$
3) a) $(x + 2)(x + 3)$; b) $x = -2$ or $x = -3$
4) a) $(x - 6)(x - 4)$; b) $x = 6$ or $x = 4$
5) a) $(x - 4)(x - 3)$; b) $x = 4$ or $x = 3$
6) a) $(x + 4)(x + 4)$; b) $x = -4$
7) a) $(x - 1)(x - 1)$; b) $x = 1$
8) a) $(x - 5)(x - 2)$; b) $x = 5$ or $x = 2$
9) a) $(x + 2)(x + 1)$; b) $x = -2$ or $x = -1$
10) $(y + 3)(y - 1)$; $y = -3$ or $y = 1$

Soving Quadratics by the Quadratic Formula (pages 91–92)
Final answers are:
1) 2, -8
2) 4, -2
3) 3.236…, -1.236…
4) 0.414…, -2.414…
5) 1.35…, -1.85…

Quiz X: Learning About Quadratic Equations (page 93)
1) quadratic equation
2) second degree
3) factoring
4) formula
5) standard form
6) numbers
7) c
8) $5x^2 - 2x - 6 = 0$
9) $8x^2 + 6x + 4 = 0$
10) $(3x + 5)(2x -2)$
11) $(3x +4)(x + 5)$
12) $(4x - 3)(x + 2)$
13) -2, or $\frac{1}{2}$
14) -3, -1